Dad,
    The late[st]
for someone who likes
to keep up-to-date!
        Love,
        Lorrie 'n Harry
        — M. Patterson

Christmas '78

A Precious Legacy

Christian Science comes to Japan

by EMI ABIKO

Published by
E. D. Abbott Company, 181 Massachusetts Avenue,
Boston, Mass.

Design by Marilyn Knudson

to Mrs. Miyo Matsukata

who helped to establish a firm foundation
for Christian Science in Japan

Acknowledgment

I am deeply grateful for the loving interest and
generous assistance of Dorothea Kahn Jaffe
in the writing of this book, and for the patient
encouragement and guidance of Robert Peel in
reviewing it.

My warm appreciation goes to Miye Matsukata
who provided tapes of conversation with her
mother: and to many other friends who shared
their memories and contributed toward this
book.

Contents

Foreword

The story told so simply in these pages, with a mixture of Eastern reticence and Western relish, is outwardly modest but spiritually heroic. The author, with a foot in two worlds, has lived through most of the events she describes, and this gives to her account the value of intimacy as well as the authority of perspective.

This is not a chronicle of "missionary" activity, in the ordinary sense of the word. When the Church of Christ, Scientist, was founded in 1879 to "reinstate primitive Christianity and its lost element of healing" *(Church Manual),* Japan was still in the early stages of emergence from its long isolation. When Christian Science several decades later slipped quietly into the stream of Japanese life, its impetus was not an evangelistic program but a healing ministry. This little book records some of the results.

The ultimate aim of Christian Science reaches beyond the regenerating of individuals to "the healing of the nations." I recall a conversation with one of the Emperor's brothers in the first year of the allied occupation of Japan. Pointing to the masthead of *The Christian Science Monitor,* which we had been discussing, he asked: "Why do Americans love the word *science* so much? Why is it needed in that title, for instance?"

When I had explained a little of the meaning of the term *Christian Science,* the Prince replied: "Ah, that makes sense! If Christianity is something that really can be applied scientifically to every aspect of human life, then the word belongs there."

His statement points to the future possibilities as Mrs. Abiko's story points to the past trials and triumphs of Christian Science in Japan. It is a story with an open-ended promise.

ROBERT PEEL

Japan fifty-five years ago

This book attempts to tell a simple story about a few Japanese families who became interested in Christian Science when this religion was still quite new in the United States. As the eldest of the children of these families, I am writing what I remember as a participant, adding what has been told me first hand by others who belonged to the small group of pioneer Christian Science families in Japan. I am telling this story in gratitude to our Japanese mothers who accepted Christian Science when it was presented to them and gave us an unusual English education. With the help of a remarkable American educator who lived in Japan for thirty-five years, they made it possible for us to read and understand the Christian Science textbook, *Science and Health with Key to the Scriptures* in the original English of its author, Mary Baker Eddy.

Before I start telling the main story, however, I must give a glimpse of what it was like

1

to live in Japan fifty-five years ago. I will do this from my own childhood memories and impressions regarding my immediate surroundings, and leave the more serious studies to scholarly writers.

My recollections of Japan begin in my early school days. My parents, both Japanese, had moved to New York City for business reasons and I was born there. Before I reached my teens my parents decided to return to their home base and I had my first view of my ancestral land. I shall never forget my initial impression at the dock when we landed in Yokohama. A long row of *rikishas,* with orange-colored rugs for footrests, waiting for us to disembark. How eagerly we children looked forward to riding in one! However we ungrateful youngsters were disappointed; our grandmother had sent her chaffeur-driven car to meet us. We had to ride in her American Packard!

In those days most of the well-to-do Japanese families had private *rikishas* and *rikisha-men* according to the size and need of the family, and our family possessed these vehicles. Private *rikishas* had family crests painted in gold on the back of the vehicle, and the *rikishamen* wore uniforms with the family name woven in white on the front of their heavy cotton navy-blue happi-coat, and on the backs a large family crest in white. They were strong, fast-running men.

2

When it was necessary to climb a steep grade they would pull the *rikishas* from one side of the hill to the other in zigzag fashion, and we would lean forward to make it easier for them. Going down we would lean backward to cooperate with them. Not everyone could pull a *rikisha;* one had to be experienced like an athlete to do it easily and gracefully. Sometimes if the rider was a very heavy person or the *rikisha* was a double-seated one, carrying an adult and child or two children, an extra man would push from behind and run with the one pulling it.

Very few families had imported automobiles, and those who possessed them usually had a uniformed chauffeur. Some had an assistant in uniform who rode beside the driver. The driver's section and the master's section were divided by a glass window. The glass did not open, but a telephone connected the two parts. An aide or a maid riding with the master or the mistress of the house used the jumpseats. Even if the car was empty, the servants would ride on the jumpseats.

Life was very formal for some families. The houses of the well-to-do were huge. We used to get lost in our grandmother's mansion.

It had two parts. One was of French Renaissance architecture with high ceilings and a great ornate stairway. The formal parlor had large chandeliers and the furniture was all

3

white and gold. The dining room had a huge table and a large fireplace. The other part of the house was in the Japanese style with endless halls from which opened several rooms. These were divided by sliding doors of wood or *kara-kami,* a laminated Japanese paper with beautiful hand-painted murals.

When the doors were all opened, the smaller rooms became one huge one to entertain guests. At the end of these rooms was a special platform for professional Noh-dancers who performed for special occasions.

Much attention was given to landscaping. The garden in front of the Japanese part of the house was a traditional one in the Japanese style, with rocks, trees, shrubs and a miniature water-fall trickling down into another garden at a lower level. The garden in front of the Renais-sance section of the mansion was beautifully kept with neatly clipped foliage and smooth lawns. A bronze fountain played at the center. At one corner of the garden two majestic storks had their abode in a huge cage which enclosed a small pond, providing the birds with a daily ration of fishes.

At the end of the Japanese building was a small inner garden which led to the family wor-ship room where Buddhist ceremonies were held. A certain temple would be engaged to watch over the ancestral rituals, and the priest would

4

inform the family when to have a ceremony for which ancestor. Most of the time it would be to remember someone of the last one or two generations, but I shall never forget one ceremony which was for someone who had died three hundred years before. Yet the priests and the family seriously followed the tradition with beautiful flowers and extravagant refreshments for the relatives and friends who gathered. It was too strange; I could not understand these adults!

Families like this had a great number of servants of all grades. The upper class servants included the dignified elderly men who watched over the finances of the household; the elegant head-maid who served for many years; and young girls from good families in the country who waited on tables and did light work as their premarriage preparation. Then came students who went to school but worked early in the morning and in the evening; and the lowliest category of servants who did heavy work inside and outside the house.

This formal living seemed very strange to a child like me who was used to living in a New York apartment or a summer house where the nextdoor neighbor was in calling distance. I felt like an alien.

I started in first grade without knowing any Japanese, because I was born and raised in New York. Without learning the Japanese lan-

5

guage, I was put in school two months after the family had moved to Tokyo. The teacher tried to say some English words, but I could not understand her pronunciation. How was I to know what "kyatto" (cat) and "doggu" (dog) meant? But the most baffling thing about my first year in school was that I had to bow to certain girls when I passed them. Even the teachers did. There were eleven of these girls in different grades. They came in their own *rikishas* and rode inside the school gate, but we had to get out of our *rikisha* outside the gate. And a nicely-dressed lady followed each one of the girls in a separate *rikisha*. At assemblies these girls walked to the front row, the older girls first and the little ones following them. They sat in different sized chairs upholstered with brocade, but we had to sit on wooden benches. I finally learned the reason for this strange procedure: these girls were princesses of several imperial families, related to the Emperor and Empress.

This school, called the Peeress School, had been established by Empress Meiji for the daughters and granddaughters of titled men. Because my grandfather on my father's side was a baron I was eligible to attend. My parents really wanted to send me to a school where English was taught every day, but my grandfather insisted on this one because he thought I was too Americanized and needed training.

6

Each year at the graduation ceremony, the Empress came and sat on a very high platform. I remember the principal telling us first graders, who were sitting behind the row of princesses, that we should put our hands on our laps in the form of a triangle and keep our eyes on the triangle, because if we looked up at the Empress we would go blind. No American child could believe that, and I peeked. I found that when the graduating girls made three very low bows to the Empress, she responded with very light bows which could be detected only because the broad rim of her hat moved.

At school I was the only one who wore western clothes, and had short hair, and wore bobby socks with my bare knees showing. The school girls' custom was to wear Meisen-silk kimonos of blue or purple with silverish symmetrical designs. The kimono was made short, about five inches below the knee, and a maroon or red skirt, a midi-length *hakama* was worn over it to make the movements easier. The girls could run and jump and be as active in this school uniform as if they were wearing sailor suits or jumpers. On a festival or some kind of memorial day, they wore purple ceremonial *kimonos* with their family crests and longer *hakama* than usual. Their hair neatly tied or braided, reached below the middle of their backs.

Most of the girls commuted in *rikishas*.

7

I went to school with a cousin, sitting on her lap in her *rikisha*. She was in the sixth grade when I was a first grader. There was a place on our way that I dreaded. It was in front of a barber shop and the same girl would always wait for us, and stick her tongue out at me and call me "the foreign pussycat." I was always made aware that I was not like the other children.

My grandparents on my father's side were active Buddhists. As we lived on the second floor of their big house for a year or so, my sister and brother and I used to follow all their customs without knowing what we were doing. Grandfather would get up before dawn, wait for the sunrise and clap his hands several times and worship the sun as it rose beyond the pine tree at the end of his garden. After that he would worship his Shinto god standing in the worship room, and then sit on a satin cushion on the floor and do his ceremonies to the Buddhist shelf which was under the Shinto shelf. We thought that was great fun and followed him around and copied him.

There were many Buddhist ceremonies in this household, but we were called "the children of America" and were excused from having to sit through the ceremonies. Our feet would go to sleep, because we could not sit the Japanese way. Three cushions each were given us and we were able to sit on them as chairs.

8

We were exposed to a lot of Japanese traditional customs, but our having been born and raised in the United States made our relatives expect us to be different. They were more educated than the average Japanese. Some of them had been abroad. My grandmother on my mother's side had many western acquaintances,—business families and missionaries—and she was quite westernized. They were all tolerant people.

If I have written so much about my own family, I have done it because I know its customs and culture firsthand. And I feel my reminiscences give some idea of the society to which the first few Japanese families belonged and by whom Christian Science was first accepted in Japan.

The earliest period

About 1917 Christian Science was quietly introduced into Japan. It came individually to three Japanese women through three different channels.

One of the women learned of it in Tokyo through an American missionary who was healed through Christian Science treatment. Another was taken by an American friend to a Christian Science lecture given in the American sector in Yokohama. The third witnessed a healing of her maid through Christian Science while living in New York City. All became students immediately.

To take up Christian Science in Japan was not easy. Family relationships among the Japanese are very close and strictly patterned; ancestors are revered and family traditions and faiths are proudly preserved. The male members, especially the head of the family and the eldest son, have special places of importance. Departure from this tradition is generally frowned upon. Thus to take one's stand in 1917 as a student of Christian Science, a religion which challenged many rigid customs, required courage as well as tact, patience, wisdom, and love.

The three pioneer Christian Scientists had an abundance of these qualities. And each one took her stand without hesitation. But each was led to Christian Science by a different route. First of the three was Mrs. Sute Mitsui, my grandmother, a member of the well-known Mitsui family, who lived in a milieu of wealth and comfort. She was frail and under a family doctor's care, but she yearned for something better than worldly happiness and was investigating various religions. After looking into a few Buddhist sects she decided to investigate Christianity. She made the acquaintance of several American and British missionaries of various Protestant denominations and learned something about their faith. One of the missionaries had to return to the United States because of illness; she was not expected to go back to Japan because of the doctor's verdict. However, she was healed through the ministration of Christian Science and returned to Tokyo, bringing Mrs. Mitsui a gift of a copy of *Science and Health with Key to the Scriptures* by Mary Baker Eddy. This missionary told her Japanese friend that her healing had been accomplished

11

through Christian Science and a study of the book. She also showed her how to study the Christian Science Lesson-Sermon based on the Bible. Mrs. Mitsui accepted Christian Science and immediately began to study the lessons daily. She was healed of her semi-invalidism and lived a happy and active life thereafter.

To appreciate the courage and devotion of Mrs. Mitsui in embracing a new religion, one must know something of her background. A leading family of Japan, the Mitsuis felt the responsibility of upholding the country's cultural traditions. For more than three hundred years its members had been closely involved in the nation's economic structure. By 1920, the eleven families which comprised the Mitsui clan, had a broad business base which included banking, trusts, insurance, export and import, ship-building and shipping, mining, department stores and other ventures. The families were closely knit; a family council watched over their affairs in finances, marriage and the education of the younger generation, especially the male members.

Mrs. Mitsui's husband, Saburosuke Mitsui, was known as a man of high morals and quiet integrity. Perhaps the most significant contribution he made was to help finance the first Japanese women's college, Nippon Joshidaigaku. His sister, Mrs. Asako Hirooka, conceived the idea of higher education for the future mothers

12

of Japan, and Mr. Mitsui supported her project in Tokyo most generously. He donated a piece of land within his large property in Karuizawa for establishment of a summer school which is still actively in use. He also provided funds for the school building.

After becoming a widow, Mrs. Mitsui led a quiet life. To her beautiful garden parties she invited acquaintances from foreign lands and Japanese business people who had been abroad, her motive being to further mutual understanding. She gave quietly but generously to worthy causes which needed financial assistance.

As a member of such a well-known family, Mrs. Mitsui's life was very formal and disciplined in the true Japanese tradition. Knowing something of the formalities, the size of her household, and the family relationships, I look back with deep respect and amazement at my grandmother's gentle courage in taking up the study of Christian Science and earnestly adhering to its teachings the rest of her life. Her social situation prevented her from being seen publicly in church, but she took many firm stands for Christianity and for Christian Science in the privacy of her daily life.

Mrs. Miyo Matsukata, the second of the triad, was of Japanese parentage but born and raised in the United States. She married a Japanese student attending Yale University,

13

Shokuma Matsukata, a son of Prince Matsukata who served as Minister of Finance and Prime Minister for Emperor Meiji. The young couple made their home in Japan. Mrs. Matsukata had been religiously inclined since early girlhood and had been searching for the things of the spirit. An American friend residing in Japan took her to a Christian Science lecture sponsored by American Christian Scientists in Yokohama, and she very naturally accepted what she heard. She became a devoted student of Christian Science, raising her children in this religion. Later she became the first Japanese practitioner listed in *The Christian Science Journal,* and has continued to be listed for nearly thirty years.

Mrs. Matsukata's life has been a story of the meeting of "East and West." Because of her New York upbringing, she was as American as any American young girl when she married into the Matsukata family. Japanese custom, especially with a family like the Matsukatas, had many traditions and formalities which were new to her. First of all, she was not familiar with the Japanese language. Moreover, she was not accustomed to wearing Japanese dresses. But her wedding trousseau prepared by her grandmother was assembled according to tradition with many beautiful kimonos and sashes and all the accessories. Her kimonos were specially adjusted to make them comfortable for this

14

American-born girl who was not used to having
layers of material heavily wrapped around her.
The procession of the bride's trousseau which
included furniture and household accessories
was said to have covered several blocks on the
way to her new home. Such elaborate wedding
preparations were still a necessary part of the
custom in the early twentieth century.

The first years of Mrs. Matsukata's life
were spent in adjusting herself to the Japanese
way of living. Her husband's family was a very
large one, but they were all kind to the new
member of their clan. Mrs. Matsukata recalls
with deep affection and appreciation the understanding and love which her in-laws expressed
toward her.

While following the family tradition of the
Matsukatas, this young woman did not lose sight
of the Christian standard for her own family.
Soon after their marriage, Mr. Matsukata was
transferred to Taiwan on business, and the
couple lived there for a short time. One day a
strange visitor appeared, a matron of one of the
big "geisha" houses. It was customary in those
days for these matrons to make social calls on
newly arrived business families. The young wife
gently but firmly let the matron know that she
was not welcome in the home, and the visit
abruptly ended.

The third member of the group, Mrs.

15

Tatsuo Takaki, found Christian Science while living in New York with her husband and children. Their Japanese maid fell seriously ill and seemed in a hopeless condition for many weeks. Learning about Christian Science from a friend, Mrs. Takaki took the maid, with her consent, to a Christian Science practitioner. The healing came in one treatment. Soon she enrolled her children in the Sunday School of First Church of Christ, Scientist, New York.

When her husband, Shunzo Takaki, passed on in New York, Mrs. Takaki returned to Japan where she found her own mother, Mrs. Mitsui, studying Christian Science. She felt this coincidence was evidence of God's direction, and took up the study herself.

About 1923 or '24, Mrs. Takaki was appointed by the Ministry of the Imperial Household to serve as a special lady-in-waiting to the Crown Princess, now the Empress of Japan. Her main duty was that of an official English interpreter when the imperial couple gave audience to foreign dignitaries or when there were palace banquets for the heads of states. Her background, education, experience and her character qualified her for this high position.

Mrs. Takaki served the imperial family for thirty-five years, accompanying them to various official functions, spending vacations with them at the several imperial villas, advising the

Empress about her wardrobe and the education of the children, and supporting the imperial family through national crises. She was a greatly trusted member of the Court. She was of few words but steadfast and with unswerving courage at difficult times.

One day, after World War II, the Empress asked her what it was that gave her such calmness and confidence at all times. Mrs. Takaki replied to Her Majesty that she was a student of Christian Science.

Although Mrs. Matsukata knew English well from her long residence in New York, the other two students of Christian Science needed help in order to understand *Science and Health*. They received it from another Christian Scientist, Miss Florence E. Boynton.

A California school teacher, Miss Boynton had come to Japan as a tutor for the children of an American family. After the family returned to the States, she stayed on and taught English lessons privately to Mr. Matsukata, to Mrs. Mitsui, to Mrs. Takaki and several others who had become interested in Christian Science and wanted to study the textbook in its original language. (There was no translation at that time.) They also desired to have their children read and understand *Science and Health*. So they engaged Miss Boynton to teach them English in connection with Christian Science.

17

This was the soil which was being prepared to receive the seed of Christian Science in Japan.

The seed needed cultivation because radical changes in thinking were necessary. But the planting flourished. Serious students of the religion found that age-old beliefs and habits fell away from them little by little as they accepted the simple truths of Christian Science.

One such experience was that of a member of a family which had a special medicine believed capable of healing diseases that even doctors had given up. This was a small but very expensive gold pill believed to be made from a bear's liver. Members of this family carried these pills constantly for protection. As one of them began to study English and learned something of Christian Science, the longstanding custom of carrying the pills left him. It simply no longer occurred to him to use them. Also the habit of relying on massage to release bodily tensions — a very common practice in Japan — dropped from him.

Another experience was that of a mother overcoming her fear of family criticism. The sister-in-law of this large family was extremely proud of the family status, and this became evident during a period of epidemic. Since the disease was associated with unsanitary conditions, she felt it would be a disgrace if any of

18

the members caught what she regarded as a vulgar sickness. So when the three children of her Christian Science sister-in-law came down with it, their young mother was almost as concerned about displeasing her relatives as she was about the children's condition. However, she was ready to rely on Christian Science help. All three youngsters were healed in a short time with the aid of a practitioner. The sister-in-law never even had to know that these children had been victims of this disgraceful illness!

The father of these children had a similar experience when struggling with a severe case of eczema which did not yield easily. The grandfather, head of the family, knowing of the condition sent a message saying that it was his wish that his son have medical attention. According to the Japanese social structure this was literally a command, not to be questioned. However, the children's father replied that he wished to rely on Christian Science help. It was a big thing for a son, to risk the displeasure of a father, and none of the brothers would dare to do so. The healing was soon accomplished.

In another family, three children came down with measles. The widowed mother and the children were living with relatives, the family of the father's eldest brother, who was a well known medical doctor. The doctor was sent

by his mother to see how the children were
doing, but he knew they were being helped in
Christian Science. This uncle of the children
came to their room in his doctor's white uniform,
carrying his stethoscope, but all he did was to
cheer up the children with some stories. He left
them saying, "Your grandmother will be happy
to know that you are all in good spirits." This
doctor had studied for many years in England,
at Cambridge, and the eldest of these children
still remembers this incident with fond respect
for the gentlemanly uncle. The measles disappeared in a very short time.

Private schools in Japan had annual
physical check-ups for the students of the entire
school. These children of Christian Scientists
were trained to be quiet about their religion,
going along politely with the school doctors'
check-up, and yet prepared not to take in the
fears and concerns expressed.

As these families were slowly but surely
growing in their understanding of Christian
Science with Miss Boynton's help, three more
families were added in the early days. Some of
their children and grandchildren are now active
members of The Mother Church and of branch
churches in Japan and in the United States.

Mrs. Mitsu Yajima, a member of one of
these families, was raised in a Japanese Christian
family and was married to a businessman with

a similar background. She was a classmate of Mrs. Takaki in the first women's college in Japan. They both lived in New York for several years and the children grew up together, in New York as well as in Tokyo. Mrs. Yajima's only child was among the children who were in Miss Boynton's English classes with the two older Matsukata children and the Takaki children.

Mrs. Yajima was introduced to Christian Science by Mrs. Takaki, and received help from Miss Boynton when she was suffering from influenza. She soon began to visit Miss Boynton regularly, and, with Mrs. Matsukata interpreting, she took up the study of Christian Science. Around that time, her little girl, Yuri, came home from school with a broken collar bone and with a bone-setter's verdict that she would have to stay out of school for three weeks. Mrs. Yajima asked for Christian Science help, and without having the bone set, the child was promptly healed and back in school in three days.

The next to join the group were two daughters of Mr. Chonosuke Yada, a Japanese diplomat. Mr. Yada and his wife were Buddhists, but the daughters were placed in a Christian school while they lived in Canada. They spoke English fluently and became loyal and dedicated members of the group. The older daughter, Mrs. Fumi Oka, who was married to a prominent businessman in Tokyo, was introduced to

Christian Science by Mrs. Matsukata. Although it was customary for Japanese boys of well-to-do families to be sent to good schools and enter one of the few famous Japanese universities in order to be succesful in life, Mrs. Oka chose to send her son, Takashi, to be tutored by Miss Boynton along with the younger Matsukata children. Later, these children attended the American School in Tokyo, and some of them attended Japanese schools for several years before going to Principia College and other colleges and universities in the United States. The younger daughter of the diplomat, Miss Kiyo Yada, also became a staunch Christian Scientist. After World War II, she followed Mrs. Matsukata's example and became an authorized public practitioner of Christian Science.

Another woman who launched her family in Christian Science was Mrs. Nobu Imai. She became interested in receiving Miss Boynton's help to understand Christian Science some time after the two daughters of the diplomat joined the group. She too had spent some time in the States when her husband's business took them abroad. Today there are three generations of Imais who are active in First Church of Christ, Scientist, Tokyo.

Thus over a period of twenty-five years Christian Science quietly took root within these few families in Japan. They had a common

bond. First of all, they were acquainted with
each other as prominent families with similar
backgrounds and social standing. They had the
unusual privilege of education and experience
abroad, but at the same time enjoyed the freedom of not being the first-born heirs of these
families, with strict restrictions and responsi-
bilities to carry on the famliy tradition. They all
chose to visit Miss Boynton regularly and were
willing to take the rather rigid discipline she demanded. There were other American Christian
Scientists in the group and two or three
Japanese who became Christian Scientists while
living in the United States.

Christian Science did not spread among
the general public in Japan for twenty-five years,
but during that time the pioneer Japanese families were faithfully studying its teachings, with
Miss Boynton's help.

Church organization came slowly. A little
Society was formed in Yokohama in 1920, but
its members were Americans. It was not until
1924 that services were begun in Tokyo with
two Japanese members, Mr. and Mrs. Matsukata,
along with seven or eight Americans. Gradually
other Christian Scientists, Japanese and
American, joined the group.

Building a foundation of English

Looking back over this brief review of the planting and growth of Christian Science in Japan, we see clearly that the movement was greatly furthered by the determination of the pioneer families to master English in order to read the textbook intelligently. As a daughter of one of the pioneers, I know first-hand how much attention was given to English instruction as related to Christian Science. For the record I am happy to recall some of these experiences here.

Japan is not a Christian country, and its language is entirely different from those of any Christian countries. It was very natural that Christian Science first came to the few Japanese who were exposed to English.

All three of the first Japanese Christian Scientists had American experience or relationships. Mrs. Matsukata's father, Mr. Ryoichiro Arai, at age 21 was one of the first Japanese young men to go to New York to open trade directly with America, thus helping to break the stranglehold that the resident Western traders had on Japanese foreign trade. That was in 1876. Mr. Arai specialized in the silk trade. He was known for his persistence, honesty and integrity and did much to build a firm foundation of mutual trust for the Japanese-American silk trade in New York. The high-level relationship between the two countries which grew out of his ethical standards resulted in a trade that greatly prospered over the years. Thus Mrs. Matsukata was born and educated in the United States.

Mrs. Mitsui was socially acquainted with American business people. Her sons were sent to Dartmouth College and Tufts College, and one of them went to Massachusetts Institute of Technology.

Mrs. Takaki also had early American contacts. Her husband had graduated from the University of Pennsylvania, and he was with the Mitsui Bussan Co. Ltd. when he lived in New York with his family.

It was natural for these women to go on improving their knowledge of English in order to have their children brought up bilingually. At this time, an ideal teacher appeared on the scene. It was Florence E. Boynton, whose career will be detailed in a coming chapter.

Several friends of these three women became interested in Christian Science and wanted their children, too, to learn English. Miss Boynton had Saturday afternoon classes for about fifteen children. It was not only a time to learn English, but also to be exposed to the freedom and joyous expressiveness of the American way.

The children of the families that were most seriously interested in Christian Science had English lessons three times a week. I was one of those children.

We would all go from our Japanese school to Miss Boynton's charming little house. It was a typical Japanese dwelling, with a small garden. The gate was at the end of a side street, and white flag stones led to the entrance of sliding glass doors with wooden bars and frame. A bell on the inside of the door rang as the door was opened.

The interior was a simple Japanese home with *tatami* (straw mats) covering the entire floor. Miss Boynton had placed beautiful rugs over the matting and had furnished the rooms with tables, chairs, and a piano. The living room and the dining room opened to her garden which was well cared for by a gardener. An old-fashioned stone basin was used as a bird bath. A large Empress tree shaded the house, and flowering shrubs gave the garden seasonal changes. The house and garden were set high above the city streets — a quiet and charming retreat.

26

The lessons, entirely in English, were closely related to Christian Science. Some of the first ones were to read and write "God is good," "God is Love," and "God is Truth." For singing we learned the hymn "Shepherd, show me" by Mary Baker Eddy. For recess, Miss Boynton made jigsaw puzzles of postcard scenes of The Mother Church, The Christian Science Publishing Society, Mrs. Eddy's homes in Lynn and Chestnut Hill, Massachusetts, and her New Hampshire birthplace in Bow.

It was a rare international group of youngsters who came to Miss Boynton's classes. In the earlier ones there were two or three Swedish children whose parents were Christian Scientists. We Japanese children spoke English and the Swedish children spoke both English and Japanese. Often we were invited to parties given at American and British homes, and Miss Boynton gave parties, too. At one Christmas, she had us children prepare a party for our parents. We were accustomed to receiving many gifts from Santa Claus, a custom of some of the westernized Japanese, but Miss Boynton brought out a sense of giving rather than receiving at Christmas time. We learned how to decorate a small tree in her garden with fruits and nuts to feed the birds. We also were taught how to make cards for our parents.

As we children grew, the number lessened,

but the children of four families continued to be prepared more and more for the study of Christian Science. These pupils learned to read the passages from the Bible and *Science and Health* found in the weekly Lesson-Sermons in the *Christian Science Quarterly*. Two sections of each lesson was the assignment for reading. Each pupil had to read part of the sections out loud. Also, each was asked to bring one passage from each section which meant most to him, with a summary for each section. Words had to be looked up in the dictionary.

From 1924 on, Christian Science services were held in Tokyo, but the small band was made up mostly of American Christian Scientists. When the Sunday School started for the first time, these children were well prepared to join it. We early learned to attend Sunday School regularly, to put first things first and give up Sunday outings with other children, which were the custom in those days. We learned what it meant to be different from others, to be quiet about Christian Science, and yet to stand for it.

During the summer vacations, these families went to the same resort, and Miss Boynton stayed at the Matsukata summer home. She gave English lessons twice a day, one in the morning around eight o'clock and another in the afternoon around four-thirty.

The Christian Science group in Tokyo did

not hold services during the midsummer months, so on Sundays the children took turns being First and Second Readers at home. They marked their books with soft charcoal sticks and colorful narrow ribbons, as they had no markers as we have them today. They had practiced reading during the week with Miss Boynton and they read well. The families attended these services and they were inspiring experiences.

It was about this time that our interest in The Principia started. Around 1924 or '25, Mrs. Frances Thurber Seal, who was one of the first to introduce Christian Science to Germany, visited Japan and stayed at the Matsukata home in Tokyo. Mrs. Seal told the family about The Principia, a school for the sons and daughters of Christian Scientists, and showed them catalogs and yearbooks. The older children began to dream about attending this school, because it was not easy to be Scientists in a Japanese school with old, binding traditions. In 1929, the first two of us from Japan went to Principia as seniors in high school. Others gradually followed, and eventually all of Miss Boynton's pupils went to Principia.

Most of these children are now active Christian Scientists in Japan and in the United States. Some have married and some have found other careers. Two of them are practitioners listed in *The Christian Science Journal*, one is a staff correspondent for *The Christian Science Monitor,* six have served as branch church Readers in one country or the other. I have been a translator at The Christian Science Publishing Society, coordinating the work with the committee in Tokyo, which includes my two sisters. One of these sisters has recently been made a teacher of Christian Science.

Feeling God's protection

The period of the earthquake of 1923 was an unforgettable time for these early Japanese Christian Scientists. Each one learned through his own experience how God protects His children when they trust in Him.

The summer vacation of 1923 began with the usual happy and busy time for the Matsukata and Takaki children in Kamakura, a seaside resort. Miss Boynton was staying at the Matsukatas' and the children had their lessons everyday, one in the morning and another in the afternoon. After each lesson, they all went swimming. The house was right on the beach.

This happy routine of learning and playing was suddenly disrupted on September 1, when a great earthquake struck the Kanto area — Tokyo, Yokohama and their wide surrounding areas. It was noontime. The Matsukata family with Miss Boynton were at home, except for one of the little girls who had gone on an errand, and the English governess who was still on the beach with her friend, an Englishwoman married to a Japanese Count.

The earthquake came suddenly and violently. It was said to be the most severe quake in seventy years! The walls swayed back and forth, and the floor went up and down. Mr. Matsukata was in the livingroom. "What is this? Is it the end of the world?" he cried. Mrs. Matsukata was there also and said, "No, it is an earthquake!" One of the children tried to run toward her parents but fell down.

Mr. Matsukata, remembering that tidal waves would follow a great earthquake, went out to call the governess, who was on the beach, to run home. Houses were collapsing, a large portion of a hill could be seen sliding into the sea, and the earth kept trembling, but the governess and her friend seemed too busy in conversation to take notice. Finally, the governess came home. Imperturbably English, she wanted to change her clothes before leaving the house, but there was no time and she was rushed to join the family. The little girl who had been sent on an errand earlier was walking through a narrow alley when the earth suddenly shook and the houses on both sides of the alley came down. She ran out to the main street where there were splits in the ground, and then to the beach, joining the family just in time for the departure.

As they were leaving their gate, the sea

water had reached their house. The fisherman who lived behind the house was standing outside his own house, which had already collapsed. Yet in his usual manner, he bowed and expressed concern and regret about this disaster. They all walked inland, and the English governess, rising to the occasion, sang one of the hymns, "I walk with Love along the way.'

At the Takaki home, about a mile inland at the foot of a mountain, the children were all home. The plump little maid had made her bow to announce that lunch was ready, when the sudden earthquake threw her on the floor and rolled her to the side of the room. She got up, and dutifully bowed again to repeat her announcement. Before she could speak, the next quake shook the floor away from under her feet, and she rolled again to the other side of the room. The eldest girl, 13 years old, kept declaring aloud, "God is Love. God is Love." The brother, who was an avid reader, simply crawled under the wicker chair and continued his reading. The plaster on the walls kept crashing down with each quake, clouding the room with white dust. An American school teacher who was staying with the family was knocked about upstairs, but managed to come down with cuts and bruises. Horrible squeaks and huge thumps were heard outside, and the beautiful old pine trees some hundred years old fell from the mountainside and big rocks rolled down the mountain into the narrow backyard. One huge rock rolled right to the house but stopped one foot away. This rock later became the talk of the town, because it was considered something of a miracle that it could stop there.

In small groups of two and three, the Matsukata family, Miss Boynton and the English governess arrived at the Takaki home. They all waited for the safe return of Mrs. Takaki who had gone to Yokohama to see off a friend sailing for the United States. She had originally planned to have lunch in Yokohama, but was led to change her plan and took a train which was just leaving the station. It was to be the last train safely out of Yokohama before the city was laid in ruins by the earthquake and burned to ashes by the fire that followed. The train had almost reached the next station when the earthquake derailed the engine and over-turned all the cars except two. Mrs. Takaki was in one of the two. She helped the other passengers caught in the overturned cars, and then walked all the way from Hodogaya to our home in Kamakura, some twenty miles, hearing rumors of fire in Kamakura and many other dangers. The group at home was enormously relieved when about 8 o'clock in the evening, they saw her walk up the hill in her usual calm and assured manner. She even carried a box of

34

sweet rolls all the way from Yokohama, because she had promised them to her children.

The earth quaked in various degrees of tremor at different intervals for three days or more. The entire group of eighteen slept in the living room and dining room with all the doors and windows open. Excited and fearful people came running up the hill with strange rumors of violence and of shortages of food and water. The atmosphere was tense with uncertainties. Communication completely broke down. A concerned relative in Tokyo sent a messenger on foot to Kamakura to establish contact with the family. He arrived with a gun on his shoulder, and told of his narrow escape from the excited and misled mob which thought he did not look like a Japanese. Wild tales of foreign invasions were heard. But the little group on the hill ordered its life according to the situation. Mr. Matsukata positioned himself at the gate, protecting the family as well as reassuring the bewildered passers-by who were running away from rumors and fears of danger. Miss Boynton and the adults spent much of the time in prayer, and the children learned to help with the simple community living and to adjust to the temporary rationing of food.

After about ten days, cargo trains were carrying passengers to Tokyo. Each passenger was allowed to carry only one bag. The thick cloth of the draperies at the beach-side house of the Matsukatas which were ruined by the tidal waves came in handy. The older girls helped sew up the bags, prepare lunches for the group, and they all went back to Tokyo.

Both families were grateful to find their homes and their servants safe. The schools did not open for some time for many were damaged or burned, and arrangements had to be made to accomodate all the children. This waiting period at home was used for new experiences for the children. The adults gathered at the Matsukata home for relief work, knitting and sewing. A couple of the older girls could knit, and the younger ones learned to knit scarves and simple sleeveless sweaters for the winter needs of those who lost everything in the fires.

Miss Boynton used this opportunity to teach the children self-discipline, orderliness, neatness, creativeness and patience. All through the disrupted summer vacation into early fall, these children had many new experiences and learned much.

Help from the United States and other countries arrived in a short time. Among the first gifts from abroad were portable pre-fabricated houses, clothing and canned goods from The Mother Church in Boston. The Christian Scientists, both American and Japanese, worked together to distribute the supplies to those in

need. Money was received from The Mother
Church too, but none of the Japanese Christian
Scientist lost all their belongings by fire, so the
money was used to help those really in need.
The church services were held in one of the pre-
structured houses also supplied from Boston.
It was the first time many of these Christian
Scientists in Japan realized the closeness and
love of The Mother Church.

Florence E. Boynton

In the history of the coming of Christian Science to Japan, the work of Florence E. Boynton, a San Francisco school teacher, runs like a golden thread. It is impossible to describe the pioneering days of Christian Science in this eastern country without mentioning again and again Miss Boynton's name.

For some twenty years she worked devotedly and successfully for the Cause of Christian Science in Japan.

Before coming to the Orient in the early 1900's, Miss Boynton was principal of an elementary school in Belvedere, California, also teaching the upper grades. Her work was highly regarded in the community. One who knew her at that time confirms this, commenting: "As a principal Miss Boynton was long remembered for her fairness, her dedication to the dignity of each individual. Also for her patience and humor in handling several recalcitrant students who rewarded her in loving loyalty."

38

This informant adds that Miss Boynton was ahead of her time in encouraging extra-curricular activities, continuing:

"She was instrumental in establishing one of the first student bodies anywhere. She stimulated art, gave school plays, school picnics, watermelon feasts, taffey pulls, — with our dignified principal enveloped in a big white apron stirring the sticky pot."

Then came the opportunity for her to go to Japan, a country in which she had long been interested. A business man who had observed her work as an educator was moving his family to Tokyo for a period. Wishing to have his four children continue their studies in English, he offered to help Miss Boynton establish a small school if she would accompany the family. She accepted his offer.

The little school, called "Miss Boynton's Academy", was based in the American family's home. The teacher lived with an English Episcopal minister's family in Tsukiji, Tokyo, and commuted every day by *rikisha,* arriving at 8:30 in the morning and teaching until noon.

The classes consisted of the two daughters and two sons of the business man and an English child who made her hour long trip, also by *rikisha,* from the outskirts of Tokyo.

One of the daughters of the business man recalls this period of her girlhood.

39

"It was a happy experience for all of us," she told me. "The schoolroom in our Japanese house was heated in winter by a huge iron stove. The classroom overlooked our big Japanese garden changing with the seasons — not to mention the Japanese pet monkey tied to a nearby tree (whose antics Miss Boynton held out as how *not* to behave)!

"I believe it was a happy experience also for Miss Boynton — a period of serious inquiry into the teachings of Christian Science, initiated in the States with the help of a dear Belvedere friend. My parents had a very high regard for Miss Boynton's sound approach and used to say, 'If Miss Boynton can take up Christian Science, it must be right.'"

When the American family returned to the United States, Miss Boynton remained in Japan, for a time teaching English in a boys' high school and giving private lessons in her native tongue. During this period she was making a deep study of Christian Science and soon was able to help others through her understanding of this religion.

From this time on, for some twenty years, she devoted her remarkable talent to teaching English to those Japanese who wanted to read *Science and Health,* and to their children. She also taught Sunday School and gave her services as a Christian Science practitioner.

It was during this period of the American teacher's life that her relationship with the Matsukata family was formed. Around 1920, Mr. Matsukata became one of Miss Boynton's pupils, taking private lessons in English. One winter, he recommended to Mrs. Matsukata that she invite Miss Boynton to their Kamakura home for the holidays and said, "I think she will do you much good." So she spent the vacation with them. Mrs. Matsukata says of that experience, "I shall always remember the wonderful light and joy that came to me that first morning when Miss Boynton offered to read the Christian Science Bible Lesson with me. It was as though a veil was lifted, the truth was so clear." Thus began the close association between Miss Boynton and the Matsukata family.

The American teacher lived in her lovely Japanese dwelling for several years. But when the great earthquake damaged her house in 1923, she was invited to the Matsukata home. Her presence as a member of the family greatly encouraged the serious study of Christian Science by the entire family and their friends. After her coming, the daily schedule of the Matsukatas started at 6:30 in the morning when they all gathered with their teacher-guest to sing a hymn and read a section of the Bible-Lesson from the *Christian Science Quarterly.* Mr. Matsukata had a special session with her each

41

morning. Miss Boynton would explain the lesson in simple terms and help him make it practical in his daily business challenges. Then she would give school lessons to the younger Matsukata girls and to the son of their friends, the Okas.

A born educator, she loved to bring out the good and the beautiful in everyone and everything she saw. She used to say that "education means to bring out the good which God has already given each child." Thus, even while she was teaching English she was nurturing the Christian Science movement in Japan. For she was constantly imparting in her schoolroom the highest sense of principle, love, alertness, order, and patience.

There were many healings in Christian Science in Japan during these days and most of the time Miss Boynton helped. She did not apply for listing in *The Christian Science Journal* because she knew the Japanese situation and customs and felt her mission was to gently help these Japanese families free themselves from the constricting thought — the well-meant care and concern of their traditional family system and the national mental climate which is based on Shinto and Buddhist beliefs. So she went about teaching English and explaining the fundamentals of Christian Science in a way the people could understand, and healing the sick when asked.

Whenever a child had a physical problem, she helped and showed how to be healed in Christian Science. At one time, one of the girls had several warts on her hands. A playmate whose family was medically minded told her that she should use acid and eliminate them. The girl spoke to her teacher about this.

"Do you think you can remove ugly thoughts with acid?" Miss Boynton asked her. The child began to watch her thinking each day and to entertain more good thoughts. A few weeks later the little girl noticed that the warts were disappearing. "Look, there are only seven of them. I used to have ten!" Miss Boynton answered, "Don't count them and don't talk about them again. Watch your thinking and keep only good thoughts." Some time later, Miss Boynton realized that the warts were all gone. She asked the child when they had disappeared, and the little girl answered, "Oh, those things! They went away some time ago. You told me not to talk about them again."

When the children grew up and began to go to church, Miss Boynton taught them how to give testimonies of healing in English at the Wednesday evening meetings. She showed them how to overcome nervousness or self-consciousness. At first the children wrote out their testimonies and showed them to Miss Boynton, who helped with the English and assisted them in making the testimonies simple and understandable.

I myself have reason to be grateful for her help in Christian Science. A few years before World War II broke out, when I had grown to young womanhood, I had a very serious problem. For six months, Miss Boynton worked for me and with me in Christian Science every morning. It was a time not only to pray for the healing of the situation, but for spiritual progress which continued even after Miss Boynton left Japan just before the war. Each morning, I would go over to the Matsukata home to see her. Miss Boynton did not dwell on the problem, but taught me more about Christian Science — how to think correctly and how to reverse the false testimony of the material senses. She also showed me how to think about the world situation as a Christian Scientist.

One of the things I vividly remember is her talk about true democracy. She said America has glimpsed it but we have yet to overcome, within our individual thinking, elements of fascism, communism and other isms before we can really understand and prove true democracy, which she defined as "the right and freedom of the individual to be directly governed by God." I still try to practice what she told me during that period. When the problem was solved, she

44

said to me that she had never seen such a young woman overcome a trial of this kind. I was very happy about my triumph, but she said right away, "But, my dear, you must remember that nothing has ever happened. The only thing that has happened and that will ever happen is the unfolding of the Christ consciousness." I felt as though my balloon had been punctured, but I realized Miss Boynton knew what she was saying and I made up my mind that even if it would take ten years, I would keep trying to understand this. I am glad for that little bit of humility I had at the time, for after two years I had occasion to perceive the meaning of this and I began to be totally liberated from any memory of the trial.

Others in our classes, now grown to adulthood, also recall her influence for good. Takashi Oka, now London correspondent for *The Christian Science Monitor,* comments: "Most of the passages I remember from the Bible and from *Science and Health,* which come to me instinctively in times of need, came from the Sunday School teaching I received from Miss Boynton and from Mrs. Matsukata, and from the weekly appointments I used to have with Miss Boynton. This spills over from Christian Science into literature, but it was really Miss Boynton that gave me my deep love of the Bible and a feeling for the sheer beauty of the Psalms and of other beloved books. I can still hear her retelling the story of Adam and Eve, saying, 'Adam, where art thou?' or of the burning, fiery furnace and Shadrach, Meshach and Abednego. This feeling for the oral beauty of poetry and prose is very important in children's education — once acquired it abides with you forever."

My friend Takashi also recalls with gratitude her great ability as an academic teacher. Writing his appreciation for this historical sketch, he continues: "It was Miss Boynton who really got me started in French. Every single day, around noon, we would have a dictation, and this got me used to hearing spoken French at an early age. Thanks to the foundation she gave me, French was never a problem for me when I got to college, and I also took an evening course with French professors that built on this foundation. This enabled me to work as a correpondent in French-speaking Vietnam and in Laos and eventually to become the *Monitor's* Paris correspondent."

Takashi further writes: "Miss Boynton had a unique capacity to make English or French come alive through her explanations. She was superb in a subject she called 'word analysis' which explored the origin of words, and broke down into their Latin, Greek or French original components. She has, in fact given me a life-long fascination with words and their meanings,

46

akin to the fascination others might have with
music or with paintings."

A final reminiscence from Takashi clinches
his appraisal of her teaching ability. He writes:
"While attending the Athénée Français in
Kanda, Tokyo, during the war, in the students'
lounge I overheard a couple of older men re-
living their middle-school days. One had been a
pupil at Furitsu Itchu and mentioned to his
friend the name of Miss Boynton as having been
a most remarkable teacher. I never got to talk
with these people, but was impressed that Miss
Boynton had left such an impression that a
pupil of hers could remember and speak of her
years later, in the middle of World War II."

One of Miss Boynton's special gifts was
her ability to discern a child's talent and help
develop it. For example, there was the experience of one of the little Matsukata girls who
came home from school one day with a card-
board model she had made of a house. Miss
Boynton saw in it a remarkable sense of pro-
portion, of design, of balance and beauty, — a
promise of artistic talent. As the girl grew up
her teacher encouraged her to study art, and
helped her to have formal lessons in Japanese
painting from Gyokushi Atomi, one of the best
artists of the day. Some years later when this
talented girl came to the United States she won
scholarships and fellowships at a well-known

school of art. Now as owner of Janiyé in Boston, designer and maker of original jewelry, Miye Matsukata is a recognized artist.

Miye has written her appreciation of the teacher for this sketch. "She loved Japanese things," Miye writes. "Long before the public recognized 'Folk Art' objects as collectable, Miss Boynton bought them. She was not a collector — but a person who lived with what she acquired. Now decorators are following what she did fifty years ago — such as making a lamp out of a wrought iron candlestick or a huge living room lamp out of a bottle. Mother said she used to give lessons showing the different categories of sophisticated city objects (as plates and curtains), rustic country baskets, porcelain and Yukata for country houses like Kamakura and Karuizawa. She framed stencils of fabric before anyone ever sold them."

Miye's impressions of Miss Boynton's artistic talents agree with my own. I recall that Japanese textiles pleased her, and she used them in unusual ways. She loved the blue and white cotton material which the Japanese use for Yukata, the garment worn in the evening to relax after a bath to cool off after the hot summer days' work. She had her summer dresses made from it. It was a very odd sight to the Japanese eye, but these textile dresses were becoming to her. She also liked colorful plaids which are

48

commonly used for Japanese bedding. She had
smocks made from the plaids for each girl, but
the girls felt awkward and self-conscious wearing bedding material. Their mother looks back
and says: "They would never go against Miss
Boynton, but I think the children suffered quite
a bit." One of the girls says today, "But that
was part of our character building. We learned
to be different and not always follow the crowd."

Other characteristics of Miss Boynton
come back to me. She was most generous in
helping the entire group improve its way of life.
She noticed small everyday details of conduct
and was alert, willing and loving enough to show
the better way. No matter how busy she was, she
would stop and call a child to put the misplaced
book on the right shelf. Sloppiness in appearance was not allowed, — dresses must be clean
and neatly pressed, buttons must be sewn on
properly and no temporary means with a safety-
pin was excused. She taught the children to dress
simply but well in order not to offend others, and
she was a good example of her precept. She
loved jade green, and several who remember her
speak of her black silk dress with jade green
piping around the V neck, her beautiful carved
jade pin, and the small jade ring. Her white
hair was beautifully marcel-waved.

While Miss Boynton was motherly and
warm, she was also very strict with her pupils.

She used to say, "What is worth doing must be done well." She made each experience a learning one. One of the things she taught the children was letter writing. When she had them write thank-you letters, they had to be done first on scratch paper, then when in perfect form on some lovely stationery. She loved beautiful Japanese paper and instilled the idea in her pupils that they must send the best to represent themselves and to express gratitude for something others had done for them. Miss Boynton was not a real cook herself, but she knew what was good. One of the girls recalls how she slightly resisted Miss Boynton's strictness about not "over-cooking." She says, "Miss Boynton felt strongly that the end product must be good whether it was a whole meal or a simple salad, and this included serving it attractively and never carelessly."

While strict, at the same time she could unbend graciously and she took part in the happy family life of the Matsukatas zestfully.

The family were most generous in including all who came to see Miss Boynton to learn about Christian Science. Thanksgiving and Christmas were happy gatherings at their home. Mrs. Matsukata would have her cook prepare a real American turkey dinner with all the delicious trimmings. Often she provided dainty Japanese place cards, and on them Miss Boynton wrote quotations from the Bible and *Science and Health,* for she never failed to remember her mission even at times of happy recreation. A natural educator, she would inspire harmonious, constructive, and interesting conversations. Although these were joyous times, full of fun, Miss Boynton was able to make them teach meaningful lessons.

So many of us benefited by the selfless and generous family life of the Matsukatas! One marvels that two women could work together so harmoniously in daily affairs and in bringing up the children. Miye, the artist daughter, explains this in the following reminiscences:

"The good relationship between Miss Boynton and my mother was a firm cornerstone for Miss Boynton's influence in our lives.

"It was my mother's generosity of spirit that made it possible for two women to live together in one household and to let the children be taught, guided and molded without jealousy or covetousness of the children's affections. Although my mother has had struggles within, her strongest point from the beginning has been the ability to 'let her children go.' It is also phenomenal that my father allowed two women to dominate his household. My remembrance of it all was that there was no conflict nor undercurrent of resentment.

"I never thought my mother could truly

51

operate by herself or run the household without
Miss Boynton. As it turned out, I never observed my mother's test period without her
friend because I was in college and Miss
Boynton, due to World War II conditions, was
in San Francisco. Now, as I grow to know my
mother better, I see that what I thought was an
inability to make decisions and her non-com-
municativeness, were shyness and a lack of
'savoir-faire'; underneath this appearance is true
spiritual sense, for when 'the answer' comes,
she acts on it. Should I have been in my
mother's place, I doubt that I could have let go
of my ego enough to let Miss Boynton have so
much influence over my children.

"I do not know now whether it really was
Miss Boynton or my mother that had the taste
to make the houses we lived in 'home', with their
livable and artistic surroundings. Of course,
Miss Boynton's artistic taste is undisputed, but
when I see mother's own choice of kimonos and
obis for her trousseau, I see her tastes as a
young bride were developed and sophisticated.
Miss Boynton had style — which is an imagina-
tive and artistic expression of one's personality
and so does my mother. Perhaps hers is a
quieter expression.

"In asking myself what was Miss
Boynton's influence on me, I am not clear as to
whether it was Miss Boynton or the religion she

52

advocated that was the force. This blurred impression is a compliment to Miss Boynton because there must have been little of herself in her desire to educate so many of us.

"Perhaps the greatest legacy from this household was a childhood with neither friction nor frustration, freeing me in later years from bitterness and resentment which could have crippled artistic expression."

As I recall it, a strong element in this relationship was Miss Boynton's love for the Matsukata children whom she loved as if they were her own. Always seeking and finding the good in each pupil, she had great expectations for all six of the young Matsukatas.

I remember her talking about their futures. She said: "Just because I have helped to bring them up in Christian Science does not mean all six of them will become active Christian Scientists. But I am sure they will all be useful and progressive people." The eldest daughter married a Christian Scientist, former Dean of Men at Principia, another daughter married the American Ambassador to Japan. The son became an officer in the United States Army and later a business executive dealing with affairs involving the two countries. He was considered an effective go-between, having a hand — directly or indirectly — in influencing some of the major improvements in the relationship between the United States and Japan. Miye, as mentioned before became a well known artist. The youngest daughter, Mari, was called "my prize baby," and Miss Boynton loved her as a very natural and good little Christian Scientist. When she was a teen-ager, Miss Boynton encouraged her to take sewing lessons, and after finishing college she became a fine dress designer. She married a lawyer, a Christian Scientist, and for the past several years, she has been a public practitioner of Christian Science in California. As for Tane, Miss Boynton once predicted, "She will either do something very solid and significant or go to the other extreme and do something out of the ordinary. She won't do anything mediocre."

This child's education was quite different from that of the other children. She had very little of what one would call a formal education until she went to Principia and then to Columbia University. After the war, she went home as a trained librarian, but there was no place to use her professional skills. Then one day her mother's long cherished idea of having a school to teach Japanese children English as well as to give them a more progressive education was once again in discussion. Tane stepped right in and started a school with two little boys whose mother wanted them to have a new kind of schooling. Today this Nishimachi International School has nearly three hundred pupils and teachers. The school authorities bought the Matsukata house and land as its campus and it is thriving with children of twenty nationalities in its classes. All are educated in at least two languages, English and Japanese.

The results of Miss Boynton's work can be seen in many lives today. Each of her former students and friends recognizes her contribution in a different way. To Miss Kiyo Yada, who grew up as a diplomat's daughter, it was this teacher's practical application of the ideals of Christian Science in daily living that meant the most. Miss Yada expresses her gratitude as follows:

"My first thought is how grateful I am that I was introduced to Miss Boynton as my first introduction to Christian Science . . . . . *She lived what she said.* She was sincere. It was not mere theory or pedantry. It was radical, based on God, Principle, Love, one Mind, but practical, so practical . . . . . I was thoroughly dissatisfied with and disgusted with the hypocrisy and the empty vanity of the worldly social elite. Life seemed so hypocritical and empty. I wanted none of it and I wanted to come out of it. So what Christian Science presented to me of God, through Miss Boynton, was truly a saving angel for me."

To me, as to Miss Yada, her great gift to

us was a spiritual one. As the eldest of the children in Miss Boynton's classes, I was at an age when I could appreciate what she was doing for us. She was not merely a good English teacher, she was a true educator. She knew how to bring out in us children an awareness of our God-given freedom and dominion, releasing us from the restrictions and age-old traditions without losing the good and the beautiful in those traditions. She taught us English not merely as the speech of a certain country, but as the language in which Christian Science was most accurately expressed because it was the native tongue of the Discoverer and Founder of Christian Science.

All of us children have been grateful to our mothers who had the discernment to recognize English as the best tool to understand Christian Science and who gave us the extraordinary experiences with Miss Boynton for twenty years. Most of all we are grateful for that golden thread which is woven into the story of the beginnings of the Christian Science movement in Japan — her work. It laid a firm foundation.

The Principia

Miss Boynton's foundational work in
English and in Christian Science prepared her
Japanese pupils to attend The Principia, a school
for the sons and daughters of Christian Scientists
in St. Louis, Missouri. In 1929, two girls went
to Principia as the first students from Japan.
During the next twelve years, ten students followed, and after World War II, the last of
Miss Boynton's pupils, Takashi Oka went to
Principia, making thirteen in all! Subsequently
pupils from the Tokyo Sunday School and other
young people becoming interested in Christian
Science in Tokyo followed, and today, as this is
written, twenty-nine students from Japan have
attended Principia College.

What has The Principia experience done
for these Japanese Christian Scientists?

It was a novel experience for Yuri Yajima
and me, the first two to attend Principia, as well
as for the school itself. The two of us were
most impressed by the warmth, love and friend-

liness that permeated the school. Principia had
obviously encouraged the students to learn something about Japan before we arrived, and one of
the recommended readings was *A Daughter of
the Samurai* by Mrs. Sugimoto. At every meal
table we were bombarded with questions drawn
from this book. Did we live in paper houses?
Had we seen snow? Did we have automobiles
or trains? Our schoolmates' concept of Japan
was cherry blossoms, Fujiyama, girls in kimono
and *rikishas*.

Yuri and I were given opportunities to
express our appreciation for this friendly and
loving reception. We had taken several kimonos
and the accessories and some dolls and other objects of interest. We were invited to show our
things, talk about Japan and answer questions
at dormitory parties, Mothers' Club meetings
and Alumni group meetings. And very often in
the English classes, we wrote about Japan, its
customs and its people. Although our composi-
tions were not particularly good, the teacher
made us read them to the class.

Coming from a Japanese school where the
faculty-student relationship was formal and cold,
we found that Principia's warmth and inform-
ality made us feel at home at once. The first
person who greeted us was Frederic E. Morgan,
president, who came to meet us at the station in
St. Louis. We were ten days early for the be-

ginning of school, so a place was arranged for
us at the Faculty Club, and Miss Martha Sparks
(now Mrs. Claude Hough) was our chaperon.
She taught us the American ways of doing and
saying things and took us shopping. The president and his wife (whom everyone addressed as
Mr. and Mrs. Freddie) called themselves our
American father and mother, and welcomed us
to their home quite often. We were introduced
to the other Morgans and many of the faculty
and staff members. It was a very new experience
for us to be in a big family of Christian
Scientists.

Being the first students from Japan had
its special privileges. I shall never forget the
Sunday afternoon, after the students had arrived.
We were out on the campus, and Mrs. Mary
Kimball Morgan, the founder of the school,
came out to the porch of Principia Hall. Yuri
and I were introduced to her as the first two students from Japan, and Mrs. Morgan kissed us.
After we returned to the dormitory, several girls
came to touch our cheeks and one of them said,
"You got a kiss from Mrs. Morgan because you
came from Japan. I wish I'd come from
Czechoslovakia or somewhere!" Mrs. William
E. Morgan (Mrs. Billie to the students) was
Dean of Girls, and she saw to it that Yuri and I
got as much cultural experience as we could. We
were taken to hear the world-famous pianist

Ignace Jan Paderewski, and heard him play the Moonlight Sonata with the lights lowered on the platform. We also heard Fritz Kreisler, one of the best known violinists of the day. And we saw Lynn Fontanne and Alfred Lunt in "Elizabeth the Queen." These three occasions are still vivid in my memory.

The relaxed and free atmosphere in the classes was something new to me. I don't ever remember questioning or disagreeing with a teacher in the Japanese school. Most of the learning in Japan was by memorization. Students merely listened to their teachers and answered questions. Each day we had to learn new Chinese characters from grade school all the way through high school. We memorized countless names and dates for history classes, and music teaching too was all by memorization. However, in this American school I saw that we had to think for ourselves. At first it shocked me to see the students disagree with a teacher, but I soon saw that often teachers invited discussions of individual views. I did not achieve this freedom while I was at Principia, but it continued to develop over the years. I remember at one history test, the question was on the Monroe Doctrine, and I had memorized the section under "Monroe Doctrine" and wrote it out letter-perfect, but it never occurred to me that other parts of the textbook contained the cause and effect of this doctrine. A fellow student who checked my paper said, "If I hadn't sat next to you, I would have thought you'd cheated, because you wrote exactly as the book says, but I know you didn't bring your book." This was an unforgettable incident, because it made me aware that I had never learned to think for myself.

During recitations in the classes, I learned very gradually how other students studied, and how freely they expressed themselves without much fear or self-consciousness. They could laugh at their own mistakes and not be ashamed. My English was not adequate to really progress far in the actual courses, but I did learn new attitudes and approaches. These helped me on the road to appreciating the joy of study, and were especially helpful in studying Christian Science as years went by.

Dormitory life was full of lessons on being natural and open, something quite unlike my experiences in Japan. Whenever someone complimented me on my dress, I would respond in the Japanese way of downgrading it, although I was really happy to receive praise. In the Japanese way this was being modest. It gave me such a feeling of freedom when I learned to be honestly appreciative of compliments and say, "Thank you." Gradually I learned to overcome false modesty with natural appreciation and to supplant suppression with poise. Many human relationship problems arose in dormitory life and Principia "dorms" were no exception. But to see the way they were handled in a group of young Christian Scientists was perhaps the most important part of my experience at Principia.

An experience I shall never forget occurred when I first roomed with two girls. They had both come from California and were friends. They always kissed each other good night, and I supposed that was their custom and thought nothing of being left out. About a month later, before they went to bed the two girls came to my bed and kissed me good night, and then sat at the foot of my bed and asked me, "Why are you such a different kind of Japanese? When we first arrived and found you in our room, we were really upset and went to the Dean of Girls to have her change us to another room. But now we like you very much. You are not like the Japanese that people speak about." As we talked, it became clear to me that they had been influenced by the anti-Japanese feeling in California, so I said, "If you went to Japan, my friends would ask you a similar question. They only know the Americans they see on the movie screens. They think American girls are painted-up and vulgar. They would be surprised to meet you, too."

The training at Principia was very thorough. At meal time, the boys came over from their dormitories, and at each table a 4th year (senior) boy and girl acted as host and hostess, and monitored the table manners and conversation of the younger boys and girls. The seating arrangement was changed periodically, and we became acquainted with many students. For me, it was a time to learn about the different parts of the United States and the varying kind of homes that these boys and girls came from. And I learned that there are all sorts of Christian Scientists, too. In a small group in Japan, we all thought alike, lived alike, and there was not the variety of thinking that I found in a large group of Christian Scientists at Principia. Now I felt like a little goldfish tossed out of its bowl into a big pond.

As more children came to Principia from Japan, both the school and the American children became accustomed to us. As the strangeness wore off those who came after us received no special treatment.

The Matsukata children were especially at home in the Principia environment. They had been brought up speaking English in the family, and they attended the American School in Tokyo. Thus their experiences were more or less like those of the American students. Eventually all six of the Matsukata children attended Principia.

Even before the first of the children came, the Matsukata family's acquaintance with

Principia began. It started with the gift of a rare family treasure, a set of festival dolls several generations old.

The gift came about in this way. One day, Mrs. Matsukata received a phone call from a curator of a museum, who had been asked to find a set of these dolls for the School of Nations Museum on the campus. At that time, the Matsukata children were too young to go to Principia, but they were expecting to go, and Mrs. Matsukata had planned to make a gift of these dolls to Principia some day. Here was the opportunity! And the whole set of the family treasure was shipped to the school.

It has long been the tradition in Japan for every family or every girl-child to have a set of dolls for the girl's festival on March 3. These dolls are called "Ohinasama", and they are miniature portrayals of the ancient imperial court. The two dolls at the top of the five-tier platform are in the ancient costumes of an emperor and empress seated on their throne. On the lower tiers are a pair of ancient warriors with bow and arrows, three ladies-in-waiting and five musicians with five differing instuments, and several other dolls. They are exquisitely made and dressed in colorful brocades. As part of the model of a court, lovely gold and black lacquer lampstands, trays, bowls and plates in miniature size make the bright red platforms very festive.

64

These dolls must be carefully kept in a storage room all year; and they are admired and enjoyed only for the few days before and after the festival. The set given Principia was an exceptionally beautiful and large one.

Mrs. Matsukata says: "I learned later that the dolls had come at a time when Principia was going through deep waters, and also one of the Trustees had been seriously ill. Therefore to receive the gift of dolls from a far away country from Christian Scientists was not only a great surprise to the Trustee, but the recognition of the school gave him much encouragement. It broke the mesmerism, the Trustee recovered and expressed his gratitude with a year's scholarship for the first child from our family."

This child was Naka Matsukata who was accompanied by her mother to Principia in 1930. Mrs. Matsukata recalls her visit with Mrs. Morgan in her summer home that year, and says, "Certainly we owe much to her clear thinking and strong perception and understanding of Christian Science."

While the children were at Principia, Mr. and Mrs. Matsukata were kept in close touch through their letters as well as through the monthly reports from the housemothers and letters from the Deans. They were loving and frank. Mrs. Matsukata remembers: "We were most grateful for all the interest given — some reports or letters made us happy, and others gave us much thought."

It was a great comfort to Mr. and Mrs. Matsukata to have five of their children in the United States during World War II. Here is an excerpt from a letter from Miss E. Olive Davis, then Dean of Women, to Miss Boynton who had returned to San Francisco. It tells what Principia meant to the whole family.

"Ever since the events of December 7, I have been wanting to find a moment to write you about our dear little Japanese family here and their splendid response to the demands of the hour. The FBI visited the college at once and sized up the situation very quickly, stating that Principia could be given full custody of these students . . . . .

"Of course, so far as the Principia students here are concerned, their reaction has been to bend over backwards in expressing to their Japanese friends the love and esteem which they have always had for them. Invitations to come and stay with them during the holidays, letters expressing their love and loyalty, continue to pour in from all parts of the country. It would also do your heart good to see Miye going over with one of the American students to put up and take down the American flag every day, and yesterday we had, in a very quiet way, what was, as I thought about it, a most remarkable service.

66

Mako (a Matsukata son) served as First Reader
with an American girl to an audience consisting
of one English girl, several Japanese, and a
number of Americans and we were all of one
Mind on the basis of the teachings of our dear
Leader, and the realization that 'One infinite
God, good, unifies men and nations' *(Science
and Health,* p. 340.)."

As soon as the war was over, Naka
Matsukata was married to her classmate, John
Rawsthorne, in Mrs. Morgan's home. Some
years later when John was Dean of Men, Naka
became one of the much respected and loved
hostesses on the college campus.

Takashi Oka was the last of Miss
Boynton's pupils who went to Principia College
after the war. English was no problem to him,
and for two consecutive years at college, he won
the Pittman Award for excellence in prose
writing.

Principia has surely meant a great deal to
these Japanese families. This well established
bond of love and understanding is extending to
many of the young Japanese who continue to
attend Principia.

World War II

The ominous atmosphere of the pre-war years began to be felt in the late 30's, as the Manchurian incident dragged on and the news was filled with reports of the dictatorships of Hitler and Mussolini. Japan became more and more nationalistic and militaristic as the Army gained power.

Signs of restrictions and regimentation began to invade our private lives. Intellectuals and big business executives were losing freedom of expression and activities, and uncertainties and fears were mounting. Among our small group, long-held customs began to be taken away. One of the things I remember is a ban on the ownership of private cars by women. My grandmother, Mrs. Mitsui, always had a chauffeur-driven automobile. Now she had to dispose of her elegant Italian car and buy a smaller one, but soon she could no longer own any car. For the first time in many many years, she had to walk or take the streetcar with an attendant to visit her relatives and friends. It had never occurred to us that she would have to do this in her late years.

The Matsukatas were watched by the police every Sunday morning as the family and Miss Boynton started out to church. Most of us had social contacts with Americans or other western nationals, and we often found ourselves followed by a policeman or a plainclothesman. Some of us were asked rude questions about our patriotism.

Many of the westerners began to send their families home. The anti-foreign feeling, gradual restrictions on food and clothing, and rumors of worse things to come made the atmosphere full of suspicion and uneasiness. The American government urged its citizens to return home. Miss Boynton chose not to be a burden to her government, and left for the United States in 1940. She knew her work in Japan was done, and she repeatedly told us to follow Principle, God, and not person. She also prepared us for the coming of other Christian Scientists to Japan, saying that their approach might not be the same as ours because "we all grow and situations change."

Christian Science Society, Tokyo, which was established in 1932, disbanded in 1941 when it was learned that the Japanese government would order all Christian churches to unite under the jurisdiction of the one "Christian Church of Japan." The small band of Christian Scientists began to meet privately or they continued their study quietly at home. With the absence of Miss Boynton, most of the Japanese Christian Scientists turned to Mrs. Matsukata for help and comfort, and for a while correspondence with Miss Boynton in San Francisco continued. Just before the war broke out, Mrs. Mitsui passed on, but she had the joy and comfort of receiving Miss Boynton's last letter to her. Soon the war completely cut off all private communications between the United States and Japan.

December 7, 1941, was a bewildering day! I was coming home from the Matsukatas, and all the way home the radios were blasting out the news of Pearl Harbor. We had sensed something was coming, but not this!

Christian Science services on Sundays and testimony meetings on Wednesdays continued at the small cottage in the Matsukata home. There were only seven of us, — Mr. and Mrs. Matsukata and their daughter, Haru; Mrs. Oka, her son, Takashi, and her sister, Miss Kiyo Yada; and myself. Mrs. Takaki as Lady-in-waiting to the Empress since the mid-20's, felt it was wisdom in her position to keep her religion very private. She continued to study and to see Mrs. Matsukata in place of Miss Boynton.

Mrs. Yajima, her daughter and son-in-law were living in the United States.

The little Matsukata cottage was close to the street, so the seven of us had to be very careful not to let anyone notice that meetings were being held. The Matsukata ground had three or four gates, so we entered from different gates at 15 minute intervals. Hymns were not sung but read softly during the service. Wednesday testimony meetings were particularly challenging. We prayed for inspiration to express gratitude to God and to Christian Science.

When the Doolittle planes flew into Tokyo and dropped bombs, the dream of the impenetrable island country was suddenly shattered, and those who could were urged to leave Tokyo. The seven of us went our individual ways. The Matsukatas went to their summer home in Kamakura, the Okas and Miss Yada lived outside the city anyway, and I took my children to our summer place in Karuizawa. Mrs. Takaki alone stayed in the city all through the war and commuted to the Imperial Palace.

When the Matsukatas moved to Kamakura, they confronted shortages of food and fuel. Their summer house was not equipped with gas or electricity for cooking purposes, so they had to use charcoal, and even that was in limited supply. Their efficient maid measured the charcoal to see how much of it she could use each day, and found that they would not be able to use more than one day's worth a week to cook rice. She also found that there was not enough rice to carry them through for very long. Concerned about this apparent prospect, the maid offered to return to her home on a farm where she would be cared for. Mrs. Matsukata and her daughter knew the truth that divine Love meets every human need, as Christian Science teaches. They told the maid never to measure again and that she need not return to her home. They never heard about lack again.

When the winter approached, they were faced with the problem of fuel for heating. The firewood which they brought from Tokyo was fast disappearing, and there was no prospect of getting more wood at that time. The outlook: no hot water for cooking or bathing.

Other problems of supply had to be solved, chief among them that of food. The family bought a goat in hopes of having milk. But there was no green for the goat since the place was barren in winter. And fresh produce for the family was needed as well.

Step by step these requirements were met. While Mrs. Matsukata was studying the Christian Science Lesson-Sermon one day and praying to realize that divine Love meets all needs, an idea came to her. She thought of obtaining a place that would be surrounded by large trees, a lovely vale — such as the one where Robin Hood and his men lived. Shortly after that her daughter found a place that could be purchased at a reasonable price. It truly was Robin Hood's dell. It was surrounded by a semicircle of hills and covered with trees, mostly pines. Below was an open space suitable for a vegetable garden.

The new home provided both fuel and food. The large trees, which served as a windbreak, would normally have been kept intact. However, the "American beetles" had taken over some of them and they had to be cut down. The hewn trees provided the needed wood for domestic heating and the supply was sufficient for the entire period of the family's stay in Kamakura.

The goat got her nourishment too. There was thick shrubbery in the "Robin Hood's dell" and the goat found her fresh fodder in the green leaves of the bushes. Thus she was able to provide milk.

Solid food for the family was also provided. Mr. Matsukata had studied agriculture in Tokyo as well as at Yale University, and was well versed in crop producing. He was led to answer an advertisement in the newspaper for a special form of high-yield sweet potato culture. With his background of agricultural study, he was quick to see the advantages of the new sweet

potato and immediately obtained "eyes" or buds.
He planted them in the sandy soil and the barren
ground soon became a beautiful green garden.
The gentleman who provided the potato shoots
expressed much love, said God was the provider,
and voiced his gratitude to Him. The abundant
crop of tubers, some as big as large grapefruit,
were not only enough for the family but fed
also many friends who visited the Matsukatas to
escape the continuous bombing and fire in Tokyo.
Mr. Matsukata became an expert on this special
way of growing sweet potatoes, and actively
went around the neighborhood helping others
grow them in abundance.

Robin Hood's dell also supplied beautiful
branches of flowering camelias, oranges, bamboo, etc., which made their livingroom cheerful
and attractive. During these experiences, Mrs.
Matsukata rejoiced in the proofs of Mrs. Eddy's
words, "God gives you His spiritual ideas, and
in turn they give you daily supplies." *(Mis-
cellaneous Writings,* p. 307). She often recalled
Elijah's question to the Shunammite woman,
"What hast thou in thine house?" and would
find her needs met with something she already
had at home.

Meanwhile, in the Oka family, the son
Takashi faced the challenge of induction into
the gruelling military machine. The following
excerpts from the young man's own pen tell how

74

Christian Science helped him when the call
came:

"One of my chief problems was a repug-
nance to the prospect of entering army life, almost
amounting to actual horror. From as early as I
can remember, this prospect had been hanging
over my head. It was not so much the physical
hardships as the terrific mental pressure which
I dreaded, because I felt I might not be able to
stand this pressure. However, this problem was
beautifully met through the silent prayerful
work of members of my family, and I found
that as the day of my induction drew nearer, I
became calmer and calmer instead of more and
more agitated. My brief term of service was
filled with opportunities for the application of
what I had learned, and altogether furnished a
valuable experience for growth in spiritual
understanding.

"Another big problem, in fact the biggest
problem of my life so far, was a false sense of
nationalism which is always such an obstacle to
clear and objective thinking. The first step in
my healing came a few days after I had been de-
mobilized, when I heard of a testimony which a
Japanese friend had given in America shortly
after the outbreak of war. In it she said, 'I do
not have to think American thoughts. I do not
have to think Japanese thoughts. I only have to
think God's thoughts.' These words came to me

75

as a great shock. For the first time I realized how blind I had been. I had been so busy thinking of myself as a Japanese that I had no time to think of myself as God's child. I saw — so clearly saw — that what was needed was to see things through the eyes of Principle and not of nationality. Since then, every time a narrow and limited conception came up, I have tried to correct it with a broader sense of God's universe and God's ideas. I rejoice to acknowledge that, as I have done so, I have been able to see things in their true light, to see them with a clear and unobstructed vision."

One of Mrs. Takaki's daughters, Mrs. Iku Yoroi, and her two children were evacuated to the southern part of Japan, to live with her in-laws. One day, the father-in-law heard English spoken upstairs where the evacuees were given a room, and reprimanded the mother for being so unpatriotic as to teach English to his grandchildren. The mother had been reading the Bible and *Science and Health* to the little ones. From then on, she and the children covered themselves under the Japanese bedcover and read with a flash light. Food was not so much a problem in the country, but this little family suffered from difference in life-style and points of view.

As for me, I took my two boys and was evacuated to Karuizawa where my mother, Mrs. Takaki, had a summer house. Karuizawa was a

summer resort up in the mountains, and many
of our friends and acquaintances had homes and
were evacuated there. Many of them had lived
abroad and therefore wished to continue bilingual education for their children. We formed
a small school and the mothers helped in the
teaching, training, and care of the children. It
was a very good experience for all of us, but
soon the government ordered it closed and the
children had to attend the country school. My
children had private English lessons after school
with a Canadian man. When the military police
found them with a foreigner, a plainclothesman
began to follow the boys, asking them why they
were learning English and what their mother
was saying about the war. The older boy reminded the man that Admiral Yamamoto spoke
English fluently and therefore was sent to the
Peace Conference in London after World War
I. This Admiral was a highly respected national
hero, and the military police had no word to say
to the boy's remark. But as a result they sum-
moned me to the headquarters and questioned
me for five hours. The officer who received me
was a graduate of the Imperial University in
Tokyo, a well mannered upperclass young man.
My first feeling was one of compassion for him.
This man had to obey orders and question me,
and I had no fear or resentment toward him.
For the entire five hours I never opened my

mouth except for routine answers. I simply smiled a polite smile. He interpreted it in his own way, for I was smiling a very subtle smile. When the interview was over, the officer walked me to the entrance and whispered to me, "You are a great lady. You did not say one word that the stupid sergeant could write down during the questioning. His notebook is completely blank. There will be no record of you."

All of us had many experiences of this kind during the war. We were all sustained by continuing our study according to the *Christian Science Quarterly* which we were able to receive most of the time.

During our stay in Karuizawa, we used to receive the current *Quarterly* through a Christian Scientist, the wife of the Danish Consul General. The Swedish family who used to live in Japan were back in Stockholm, and they would send one copy of the *Quarterly* to the Swedish Minister in Tokyo, whose legation building was rented from the Matsukatas. While the Matsukatas were still in Tokyo, the Minister gave the *Quarterly* to the family, but after they moved away, he would give it to the Danish Consulate, and the wife of the Consul General who was evacuated to Karuizawa would bring it to me. Then I would make seven copies and carefully send them to the Matsukatas and the Okas and to my family. This was the way we were able to study the same Lesson-Sermon with the rest of the Christian Scientists in the world. Only for a few periods we used old *Quarterlies* for our study.

The Matsukatas moved from Kamakura into the mountainous village of Kazuno in Gumma Prefecture. This was where Mrs. Matsukata's father, Mr. Ryoichiro Arai, was born and raised. Eighteen families in this village bear the name of Arai, and these farm houses are scattered far apart across the hills and valleys of the area.

Kazuno seemed so far away from the cities and so quietly primitive that it was hard to imagine that a man as urbane as Mr. Arai could have been raised here.

The old but solidly built storehouse of the Arai home in Kazuno stood by a spacious lot which Mr. Matsukata and his daughter, Haru, cultivated into a thriving vegetable garden. The storehouse was remodeled into pleasant living quarters and became a home for the family. It was to this house that the Matsukatas most generously invited me and my two boys when it became urgent for us to move from Karuizawa, because of the increased activities of the military police in that town. Haru had visited us in Karuizawa and said, "This is no atmosphere in which to rear two little boys. I'll persuade my parents to have you move to our place."

79

It was more than the usual generosity for any family to take in three more members, for most families had their hands full trying to feed their own.

The Matsukata vegetable garden must have surprised the farmers who had been working pretty much in their customary primitive way. One day I overheard one farmer saying to another, "That city girl farms with her head, while we toil with our hands and feet." They had been growing rice, wheat, barley, corn, potatoes and some conventional vegetables. Haru was following her father's agricultural textbook and sending for seeds of various vegetables.

The vegetable garden must have become the talk of the village, for one day, five or six village elders asked to be shown the garden. They were dressed in their best clothes to call on the Matsukatas, and the family cordially showed them around. At one point, the elders became very serious and told the family with great regrets that they must promptly burn away the corn patch. Each plant had a dreaded disease that could affect the entire garden. As they were telling the bad news to Mr. Matsukata, I noticed Mrs. Matsukata slipping away into the house. I had become very curious about a Christian Science practitioner's life. I had thought an hour of study in the morning was enough, and was surprised to find that Mrs. Matsukata al-

most constantly read or studied or prayed. I
followed her upstairs where she already had her
Bible open. She said, "Emi, we must know the
powerlessness of jealousy." I could not connect
the corn disease and jealousy at first, but I sat
down and leafed through my Bible and *Science
and Health,* when suddenly the light came. The
professional farmers were jealous of the city
folks' farming success! I felt this was a good
opportunity to watch how prayer in Christian
Science works. Maybe the corn disease would be
gone tomorrow? Would it simply drop off or
melt away? I watched the corn patch every day,
but the symptoms did not disappear. Instead,
something else happened. This disease was supposed to prevent the formation of corn ears, but
the ears began to appear. They kept growing,
too, and as time went on, we all enjoyed two ears
of corn from each stalk daily. They were our
main supper for almost two months! There were
many other lessons to be learned as we worked in
the garden.

Then one day, all the newspapers seemed
to have the same editorial. All papers were under government control, and we knew we had to
read between the lines for real news, but this
editorial was a command that all Japanese must
obey the Emperor no matter what he might
order. I remember saying, "I guess the war is
coming to a close," and Mr. Matsukata laughed

at my optimistic prophecy. In a day or two it was announced that the Emperor would speak to the nation through the radio. This was an unheard of thing. Speculation ran wild, one rumor was that he was going to announce the invasion of American troops and that every last Japanese must fight to his death; another rumor predicted that he would announce a negotiated peace.

On August 15, in the early afternoon, the mailman came walking up the hill. As he delivered the mail, he sat down on the doorstep, and all strength seemed to leave him, as he said, "I didn't know that our Emperor had no backbone! He's surrendered! What a sad and disgraceful day for our country!" The Matsukatas' maid relayed the mailman's news. Haru and I were elated that the war was over, but Mrs. Matsukata had a difficult time keeping us quiet and discreet. In the evening we went next door and quietly listened to the Emperor's voice on the radio. The war had ended in Japan's defeat.

This was a shock to the Japanese, who had believed that Japan could never lose a war because she had never lost one. It was unthinkable that Japan would surrender. The farmers were so shaken that none of them were seen on their farms. For three days, nobody seemed to work. Mr. Matsukata went around visiting them, gently and wisely explaining to them the wisdom of the Emperor which would prevent further fighting, killing and dying. He encouraged them to get back to work and think about bringing peace to the world. Little by little, the farmers returned to their fields.

The first news of the landing of the American troops reported that three war-correspondents had entered Tokyo, and the Christian Scientists were elated to find that Gordon Walker of *The Christian Science Monitor* was one of them.

The occupation period

Japan's surrender and the American occupation in 1945 were accepted with surprising docility by the Japanese. The propaganda of the militarists had caused rumors and concern for violent resistance, but to the average Japanese, the historic broadcast by the Emperor himself was a command to be obeyed. The American forces were not what the people had been told to expect either. The conquerors wore pistols on their hips when they first landed and entered Tokyo, but in about a month they had no need for them. One of the American officers told of his first drive from Yokohama to Tokyo when, at the sound of a jeep, mothers along the way would run out and carry their children into their houses, but in a month as he drove back to Yokohama, the children were gathering around the jeep and asking for "chokoletto" and "chu-in-gamu."

For the few Japanese Christian Scientists, the occupation period brought liberation and

progress in every way. Reading in the newspaper the name of the Christian Science Monitor
war-correspondent, Gordon Walker, Mr. Matsukata and Haru went down from Kazuno to
Tokyo to locate him. In the meantime, Lt.
Robert Peel of the U.S. Army sent a message
to Mrs. Takaki through a carefully selected
channel. He had been an instructor at Principia
College, and had taught Mrs. Takaki's daughter,
Tori, in his English class as well as in his
Sunday School class. He brought news of her
as well as news of the Matsukata children.
Although these families were sure the children
were safe during the war, it was a great relief
for the mothers to receive first hand word of
them after four years!

The group in Kazuno remained in the
village until it seemed appropriate to return to
Tokyo. During that time, Haru had located
several Christian Scientists and came with Lt.
Peel and another war-correspondent, John
Beaufort, of *The Christian Science Monitor,* to
Kazuno in a jeep. Who would have expected to
see an American jeep drive up to the village of
Kazuno! And so soon after the war!

Our isolation period as a small group of
Christian Scientists was over, and a new era of
associating with many friends from the United
States was dawning. Through these two men,
we learned news of Christian Scientists in the

outside world. They shared many encouraging and inspiring testimonies of their wartime experiences as well as what they knew about our families and friends in the United States. Some of them were teaching Japanese at Harvard, Yale, and Michigan, and others were going right on with their respective studies.

When we returned to Tokyo after several weeks, more Christian Scientists had arrived. The Wartime Volunteer Workers had started Christian Science church services in Tokyo and we were invited to attend these military services. I shall never forget the first service with a group of American military people when we sang the hymn, "Help us to help each other, Lord." We had not been able to sing hymns for four years, and now we were free to sing, and with so many friends!

Some time in October or November, a Christian Science chaplain, Major James Watt, arrived and came to Tokyo to find the Matsukatas. He was relieved to learn that there was a small group of Japanese Christian Scientists who spoke English. Many more members of The Mother Church arrived with the Occupation Forces, and the services were held in the partially bombed Methodist church on the Ginza. As winter came, the church edifice became very drafty and cold. The GI's brought a stove and each Sunday and Wednesday a box of coal to give some warmth to the bare auditorium. Sometimes mice were seen running across the floor. Nevertheless, we were grateful to have a place to hold services.

The Wednesday testimony meetings were wonderful. Officers and GI's who had fought in the Pacific theatre had outstanding testimonies of healing and of protection from extreme dangers. The wartime experiences for them were not of human will-power, animal courage, hate and fear, but experiences of steady spiritual progress in patient endurance, moral courage and universal love.

The young Wartime Volunteer Workers impressed us greatly. Our impression had been that practitioners were seasoned and older men and women, but these young men were acting as Christian Science practitioners and helping their fellow officers and GI's. It was like an open-window bringing fresh air to our idea of Christian Scientists.

As soon as Gordon Walker opened the *Monitor* office, Haru Matsukata became his secretary, and with Robert Peel and John Beaufort on hand, we were all brought closer to the *Monitor*. As subscribers to the *Monitor,* some of us had heretofore limited our interest to the religious articles and the women's and children's pages, but now we were gradually being led to become intelligently interested in world affairs.

We were particularly impressed as we watched first hand how these writers carefully checked and rechecked the facts of their stories.

Chaplain Watt said he needed a secretary, not necessarily a skilled secretary but a Christian Scientist who understood Japan and the Japanese. So without any training, I became his secretary and learned the work on the job including the driving of his jeep. I shall never forget the morning when I received a call from a hospital ship. The ship's surgeon told me that a young sailor was to have his leg amputated the following day. He was a Christian Scientist, and would the chaplain pray for him so that he could calmly face this surgery? I gave the message to the chaplain when he returned to the office. He promptly had me call up a young sailor, a Wartime Volunteer Worker, and order a boat for him to visit the hospital ship. I said, "Chaplain, but that sailor is just out of Sunday School!" The answer was, "He has learned in The Mother Church Sunday School that God is the only Healer, and he is an appointed Christian Science Wartime Volunteer Worker." That afternoon, the young man took his Bible and *Science and Health,* and went on his mission. The following morning the ship's surgeon called to report that the examination showed there was no need for amputation. He said the patient would rest awhile.

It was wonderful to meet so many Christian Scientists. The Matsukata, Oka, and Takaki homes became happy visiting spots on Sundays after church or Wednesdays before church. The American friends of the U.S. Army, Navy and Air Force brought their C-rations and K-rations and their share from the PX which were quite a treat for the Japanese, and they enjoyed the fresh vegetables and other food which were obtainable in Tokyo. Between the three homes, no one who attended the church services was left without an invitation. Unusually warm friendships were formed through these get-togethers.

Christmas 1945 was a very special occasion. The Matsukatas invited the entire group of more than thirty to their home in Kamakura. The large livingroom with a dining area was charmingly decorated with the special artistic Matsukata touch. Instead of a pine tree, a bamboo tree was decorated as a Christmas tree. The American guests brought a great deal of the food including roast turkey, canned goods and gallons of ice-cream, and the Matsukatas furnished what was available to the Japanese. It was a great Christmas party with much joy and gratitude. We all sang hymns and carols, and the conversation and discussions were very lively. It was the first bright spot in the otherwise dismal environment.

Shortly after this party, the Occupation

Forces settled into various buildings in and out of Tokyo and new temporary quarters were built. The Army Chapel became available for Christian Science services, and with special permit cards, the Japanese members continued to be invited. However, they were strictly military services, and civilians, especially Japanese civilians, could not participate in the church activities. The services were then moved to the hall of the Industry Club.

By the time this move was made, the chaplain's wife, Mrs. Ellen Watt, had arrived. She was a public practitioner, listed in *The Christian Science Journal*. Her arrival was greatly welcomed by many of the Christian Scientists in the Occupation Forces as well as by the Japanese members in Tokyo. Chaplain and Mrs. Watt rented the little house in Mrs. Takaki's garden. While the chaplain was busy in Yokohama, Mrs. Watt was giving Christian Science help at home to both the American and Japanese friends who asked for appointments.

One of the things that made an impression on me was that Mrs. Watt often talked about "doing world work," which I did not understand at the time. However, it stayed with me until some years later I found out for myself how to pray for the world.

Soon another practitioner, Mrs. Mabelle Homes and her husband, an Air Force officer, joined the group. Several other officers and Red Cross workers and civil service workers came and our church family grew. Some children arrived with their military families, and the Sunday School classes were held both in English and in Japanese.

Just as Miss Boynton predicted before she left Japan in 1941, this influx of Christian Scientists from the United States brought about an entirely new development. The war did not leave any of us, Americans or Japanese, with bitterness or hatred. There was an almost unbelievable desire to understand each other as people. One of the biggest surprises was to find that so many American officers and men, having learned Japanese during the war, could communicate with the Japanese. The Japanese have always wanted to learn English and things western, so in spite of the military suppression during the war, this desire was quickly revived. They were ready and willing to work for the Occupation Forces and learned English or improved upon what they already knew.

The Japanese Christian Scientists were still cautious about presenting Christian Science to the average Japanese, but the Americans approached new people with open arms. They freely sowed the seed. Of course, some seeds fell by the wayside, some on stony places and some among thorns, but some fell on good ground.

There were several Japanese employees of the Occupation Forces who became interested in Christian Science, and for the first time since Christian Science was introduced to the few families in Japan, the door was opened to a wider circle of Japanese. These are some of to-day's active members, all of whom have been class-taught and are serving most loyally and actively for the church.

While the group was still at the Industry Club, Christian Science Society, Tokyo, was re-established.

In Kyoto, Christian Science activity began with a handful of Americans attached to the Eighth Army in 1946. They formed a group and held services at the Army Chapel. There were no Japanese Christian Scientists in Kyoto at that time, except one person who possessed a copy of *Science and Health*.

Mrs. Midori Kadota had been a student of English in her college days, studying American literature. When her oldest son passed on, a friend ordered for her a copy of *Science and Health* from Boston. It comforted and sup-ported her as she read it during the war. After the Eighth Army made its headquarters in the center of Kyoto, Mrs. Kadota had occasion to help a Japanese friend who went to the personnel office of the headquarters. This eventually de-veloped into her working part-time for the Red

Cross library. She was overjoyed at the opportunity of once again having many books to read in English. One day she was reading her own copy of *Science and Health,* when a woman officer passed by. This officer came by frequently and they began to exchange conversation. When the officer noticed the book on Mrs. Kadota's lap one day, she brought another woman and introduced her. This was Mrs. Marguerite Bogman, who had started the Christian Science group in Kyoto and was serving as First Reader. Mrs. Kadota was promptly invited to join the group, the only Japanese attendant at the services.

Gradually the news of the Christian Science services filtered outside the Army, and a German woman who was teaching English at home brought her pupils and several friends to the services to hear English spoken and read. Two or three among this visiting-group continued to attend the services and are today members of the Christian Science Society, Kyoto.

When the American members were leaving for home, they arranged to have the services at the Y.W.C.A. where the Japanese could carry on the activities. But this did not last long, and the group was asked to move out of the Y.W.C.A. Then began the challenging task of finding the place and money to establish a permanent home for the group which was soon to become a

Society. Mrs. Kadota likens this experience to "crossing deep waters and valleys of tears" but she also says, "Somehow we felt safe in being directed by Love and by Mind."

A charming Japanese house was purchased with the generous and loving help of The Mother Church, those Americans who started the group, their friends, and many who heard about the budding venture in Kyoto. Contributions poured in from all over the United States to help this beginning of Christian Science activity in Japan's ancient capital with its historic palaces, shrines, temples and deeply held tradition and culture. First Church of Christ, Scientist, Tokyo has been of great help from the very start and over the years.

During this early period of the Occupation, several of the men and women of the Armed Forces taught English or gave talks to a group of us. It was as though we were gradually gaining a wider view of the world and recovering from the four years of blindfolded isolation.

My children were perhaps the most fortunate youngsters in Japan. They could understand some English, so they were happy to have so many soldier friends in uniform. One day they had their first jeep ride with a lieutenant who drove them behind General MacArthur's car as he left the GHQ. The boys came home exuberant that they had "chased General MacArthur!"

Just before Christmas another officer brought them a pair of Army socks, each tied with a blue ribbon. Inside one of them was an Army cap which folded up neatly, and in the other was an olive green fatigue cap. Pencils and candies from the PX were in each sock too.

These experiences opened many happy associations with our friends from the United States which continued for many years.

Several of our friends taught English to the boys. They were eight and ten, and these lessons prepared them to enter The Principia after a year and a half. Some of these tutor friends not only taught them English, but played ball with them, ran races with them, played violin with them and were perpetual gift bearers too. One sergeant used to bring them a loaf of white bread each week which the children loved, and in exchange we gave him the dark bread which was our ration. Another teacher ordered a pair of leather shoes for each boy, because they had been wearing whale skin shoes during the war.

It was a happy time for the few Japanese who had been quietly continuing their study of Christian Science. The patient and wise training given by Miss Boynton over so many years had prepared us to receive this sudden influx of

Christian Scientists from the States and to be able to associate freely with them as fellow Christian Scientists, rather than Americans and Japanese. Miss Boynton had often said, "We must first be Christian Scientists and then American and Japanese."

When Chaplain Watt's term of duty was over, many other Christian Scientists who had been such a help to the Japanese Field returned home too. The Japanese Scientists still needed help, and asked The Mother Church to let us have the Watts back or send someone else. Mr. and Mrs. Frederic Foote, both listed practitioners, were sent, and continued to help the group in Tokyo, which was reaching a new stage of progress.

Up to that time when there were many American military personnel attending the church services, Army and Navy jeeps were used by these generous people to bring the Japanese members and friends to church. Tokyo is a sprawling city and the transportation system was very poor after the war. Attending church services posed quite a problem for most of the Japanese members. However, Mr. and Mrs. Foote came with a station wagon provided by The Mother Church. Members recall with loving gratitude how much help they had received, as Mrs. Mildred Warder drove this station wagon to bring them to church and drove them home.

Mrs. Warder has lived in Tokyo ever since, and has continued to work most tirelessly and lovingly for the church. She is a well known interior decorator with a firmly established business of her own in Tokyo.

Along with Mrs. Warder, Miss Dorothy Risser, who also was with the Occupation Forces, stayed on in Japan. She too played an important part in supporting the church activities as she served in many capacities. She is particularly remembered with deep love by the Nishimachi International School where she was one of the most helpful of teachers, acting as Tane Matsukata's right hand in running this remarkable school.

In 1949, during Mr. and Mrs. Foote's stay in Tokyo, the Christian Science Society became First Church of Christ, Scientist, Tokyo, and the idea of a church building began to unfold. A committee was formed, and as the membership gathered to hold inspirational meetings and individually continued to pray for guidance, the committee found a suitable property in one of the best sections of the city. The owner expressed his pleasure in having his property transferred to a church. It was Mr. Matsukata's valuable assistance that brought about this harmonious negotiation. His business experience and his generous contribution of time and effort were a vital factor in obtaining this ground.

97

Due to postwar financial conditions, the Japanese members felt they would be grateful enough to have a very simple building. When a plan for a beautiful edifice came as a gift from an architect in the United States, it seemed much too costly for the Japanese even to dream of. At a Board meeting, however, two American members spoke out very clearly that it was just a matter of the quality of our thinking. They pointed out that a church suitable to the city should be considered. This "divine idea" began to unfold in the consciousness of the members, and at a subsequent meeting they were all asked to pray in regard to the project and meet again in two weeks' time. The result was a unanimous vote to accept the generous gift.

In Japan there are no bank loans for churches, and the church had only a few thousand dollars in the bank. However, they began to break ground, chose one of the best contractors, and hired a Japanese architect to supervise the building. The contractor worked out a plan for monthly payments, and the building progressed harmoniously. The contractor seemed to have more confidence in the Christian Science Church than the members themselves, but the demands of the situation drove the membership in prayer to God as the only source of supply.

There were many problems along the way.

At one point, when funds were almost exhausted and the church was on the verge of stopping the project, a Christian Science lecturer came to Tokyo. The Executive Board met with him and told about all the work they had been doing without success. The lecturer said, "You haven't begun!" and told them of the common human steps they could take. This broke the mesmerism of discouragement. The lecturer also spoke lovingly and firmly about the ethics of spiritual truth, which called for a complete foundation. Although the members had thought in terms of building just one wing of the plan, the idea of one complete foundation now began to unfold in their thinking, and it was decided to aim for the whole plan. The builders fully agreed.

The building was progressing smoothly and the time had arrived to put in the furnace boiler before completing the floor. The Building Committee was told by the foreman that if the furnace didn't arrive on time, construction would have to be stopped. The furnace was made in the United States and was to be shipped across the Pacific. Then came the news that a big port strike was about to take place on the American west coast. No ships would be leaving. A Japanese Christian Science practitioner reminded the members, "Our only responsibility is to see that *we* never go on strike against God." As they continued to pray, God continued to work with them. One more ship came in, and on it was their boiler furnace. No other ship came for the next three months. The building continued with no interruption.

An American member who was in Tokyo at the time says, "As the building was con structed, the workers had to be paid each Friday. One week we found we didn't have enough money to pay them. The church board and the building committee met on Thursday evening. We were rather depressed, for we didn't have a financial solution. None of the Tokyo or American banks would lend money to a church building project. We had been told that if the workers were not paid, the construction of the church would stop the next day. Mrs. Matsukata said: 'With every right idea comes the supply. The supply is within the idea.' We were truly inspired as we left the meeting, though the treasurer still didn't have the cash to pay the men. When Mrs. Takaki arrived home she found in the mail a check for $1,000 from a California lady, and this more than covered our Friday payment. We never lacked the weekly payment after that. Once we realized that the supply is in the idea, the weekly payments were always met."

Another unforgettably happy experience during the mid-50's was the activity of *The Christian Science Monitor* Youth Forum. Young

Japanese students, — some of them pupils in the Sunday School and others who were too old to attend Sunday School — had the opportunity of joining in various activities with young Americans. It was a joyful time of learning English and getting better acquainted with Christian Science. The American friends were generous with their time and effort, and the friendships formed during that period are repeatedly rekindled as they visit one another's country.

Fifty years later

Some readers of this book will no doubt wonder why devoted Japanese Christian Scientists were so hesitant about having Christian Science literature translated into Japanese. But others will read between the lines of this narrative and appreciate the difficulty of translating into the language of a people of such vastly different religious and cultural background.

Christians are a small minority in Japan. The life and teachings of Christ Jesus are little known among the people, although there are translations of the Bible into Japanese. The Japanese approach to ethics and morality is quite different from the Judeo-Christian ideals of the West. The concept of one infinite God is unknown to the average Japanese, and the highly developed sense of individual worth which has come down from the Renaissance and Reformation in Western Society is alien to a culture still dominated by the family system and consensus thinking.

102

All this is reflected in Japanese language patterns. An American born and raised in Japan, former Ambassador Edwin O. Reischauer, has written in his recent book, *The Japanese:* "Language is a fundamental tool in international relations, and the Japanese language is also a major subject in itself. It is what defines the Japanese more distinctly than any other feature in their culture. At the same time it is a major problem in their relationship with the outside world." He further explains: "Translation, however, remains an uncertain reed. Even assuming a perfect knowledge of both languages on the part of the interpreter, which is rarely the case, English and Japanese both suffer a radical transformation in being converted into the other. Word order is in large part reversed; clear statements become obscure; polite phrases become insulting; and a remark, even though accurately translated in literal sense, may take on an entirely different thrust."

The road to the first edition of *Science and Health* in Japanese translation was a long, hard, uphill one. For a long time none of us felt it was really possible to produce such a work. To begin with, there was the basic question of how to translate the word God and the seven synonyms for Deity, given in the Christian Science textbook. To Japanese thought, there are gods many, minds many, spirits many, and souls many; and there is no capitalization in Japanese writing to distinguish between God and gods, Mind and mind.

Because of innumerable difficulties such as these, the pioneer Japanese Christian Scientists thought it natural to learn English and read *Science and Health* and other Christian Science writings in the original language. To this end they had us children brought up not only to read English but to think in that tongue. Christian fundamentals and ideals were gently and patiently introduced to us as part of our education, and we learned to free ourselves from some of the binding traditional beliefs of a non-Christian country. Thus we were blessed with the privilege of being able to study the original textbook of Christian Science. Those of us who had lived for a time in the United States found this quite natural.

However, as we grew in our understanding of the universality of Christian Science, it became evident to us that this teaching should be presented to non-English speaking people, too, and their introduction had to come in a language they could understand. Unless they were introduced to this Science of Christ in their familiar speech, how would they have the incentive to learn English in order to study the inspired words of Mary Baker Eddy just as they came from her pen?

104

However, it was not until after World War II that the question of a Japanese translation came up for thoughtful discussion. American Christian Scientists who came over in the Occupation Forces asked many questions about possible translation, and as a result of their queries, we began to open our thoughts.

Yet we felt Americans just did not really understand the situation. The translation of Christian Science literature into Japanese would require a deep understanding of the metaphysics of Christian Science and of the English language, as well as some literary ability in the Japanese tongue. We questioned whether a person with such qualifications could be found at that time. Also, we were concerned about the Japanese reaction to such an effort so soon after the war, and the extremely nationalistic period which had preceded it. However, experience was to teach us that patient preparatory work would enable us to advance toward the great goal of translating *Science and Health with Key to the Scriptures* — a goal that was reached in 1976.

Our American friends were a great help in the long preparatory period. Early in the Occupation regime a group of American newspaper editors came to Tokyo. Erwin D. Canham and Donovan Richardson of The Christian Science Monitor were among this group. Mr.

Canham felt it would be a good idea to have a Japanese translation of the religious articles in the *Monitor*. This idea, voiced in 1946, was eventually carried out in the April 30, 1958, issue — the first contribution in Japanese to appear in the *Monitor.* Much had to be worked out for the publishing of this one article. While certain Japanese members of The Mother Church in Tokyo worked on the translation, groping for appropriate expressions, the problem of having it printed in the *Monitor* in Japanese characters had to be solved. During that time, a small pamphlet entitled "Christian Science, what is it?" was also translated and published by The Christian Science Publishing Society.

In 1959, a member of The Board of Directors of The Mother Church, Clayton B. Craig, made a tour of Asia to visit Christian Science groups in various parts of the Orient. When Mr. and Mrs. Craig visited Japan, they took a trip to Nikko accompanied by one of Mrs. Takaki's daughters who had returned from the States. This young woman had spent the war years teaching Japanese at an American University while she continued her graduate studies. The Craigs approached her with the idea of translating *Science and Health* into her native tongue. This was a welcome encouragement for her because she had felt the need of a Japanese translation for some time but was aware that none of

106

the Japanese Christian Scientists felt the time
for the project had come. The discussion of the
possibility of such an undertaking lasted until
two o'clock in the morning. Although the actual
translation of *Science and Health* did not start
for several years, this visit to Nikko was the
spark that resulted in the formation of a committee in Tokyo to translate religious articles
under the guidance of the Translation Department of The Christian Science Publishing
Society. The first edition of *The Herald of
Christian Science* in Japanese was published
three years later.

The beginning of this venture into Japanese translation was difficult, for most of us
Japanese church members had been studying
Christian Science in English for more than
twenty years, and we were not at all comfortable
about explaining Christian Science in Japanese.
In whatever concerned Christian Science, we all
thought in English and spoke in English. On
the other hand, the new Japanese Christian
Scientists who took up the study through introduction by members of the Occupation Forces
thought in Japanese and were still at an elementary stage of their study. All things considered
there seemed not to be the properly balanced
tools with which to launch such a project. But
seeing that the time had come to share Christian
Science more widely in Japan, the work had to

start no matter how faltering the first steps might be. As in any language, translation work brings out human opinions and human wills and the going was rough, but the vision, dedication, and courage were there.

As it has been shown in times past, God has a way of supplying the human need. The committee was greatly encouraged when a qualified young Japanese woman, Toshi Morikawa, joined the Tokyo church. She had spent several years in England as a child, had graduated from the Tokyo Christian Women's College, majoring in English literature, and had returned from the United States with a degree from a midwestern University. She had just learned of Christian Science during her last year in college. Toshi was a godsend to the translation committee in Tokyo. Our committee members, having always studied Christian Science in English, often groped in their translation effort for Japanese words to convey meanings. Now this bilingual young woman, an NHK radio commentator, brought to the translation task her special ability in Japanese.

Since then this committee has produced on a regular basis translations for the Japanese edition of *The Herald of Christian Science* and for the religious articles in *The Christian Science Monitor*. Its members have also translated several pamphlets and leaflets and a couple of books.

108

A big step forward for Japanese translation was taken when the members of the Tokyo
Church asked for and received permission of the
Trustees under the Will of Mary Baker Eddy,
to translate into Japanese the citations from
Science and Health for their study of the weekly
Bible-Lessons. These informally-translated citations were mimeographed by a committee of
local members and sent out each week to those
who subscribed for them. The Kogo Bible translation published by the Japan Bible Society was
used along with them. In about a year, the
church began to hold one Sunday service a
month in Japanese. The number of Japanese
services was increased as translators found it
possible to keep up with the weekly lesson. In
1970, the church was able to begin having weekly services in Japanese in addition to the regular
English services.

　　None of us can begin to estimate the value
of the contribution of this committee, which
worked so selflessly to provide the weekly Bible-
Lessons in Japanese for the Sunday services as
well as for the daily study of the subscribers.
For five or six years, a group of members met
twice a week to prepare these lessons. As their
consultant, Mrs. Matsukata, says: "The translation of the weekly Lesson-Sermons has been
a long and challenging work, but inspiring. It
has unfolded to many Japanese members who

served on this committee a deeper sense of what Christian Science is. This indeed was a time for real growth and understanding."

While the written Japanese translations were gradually bringing Christian Science to the Japanese, the spoken Japanese translation was also developing. In the early 60's, the testimonies at the Wednesday meetings began to be translated into Japanese as well as into English, so that all might understand. Translation of Christian Science lectures during their delivery was started about the same time. In recent years the membership meetings and inspirational meetings have also been translated.

While First Church of Christ, Scientist, Tokyo, was progressing in its translation work, and more Japanese were becoming interested in Christian Science, a special translation committee appointed by the Board of Directors was quietly translating *Science and Health*. For eleven years this committee in Japan was working faithfully and consistently. The work demanded humility, inspiration, prayer, and dedication. The offices of the Publisher's Agent and the Translation Department worked closely with the Japanese members, giving them loving encouragement, thoughtful guidance and patient help in this unique task of producing *Science and Health* with the Japanese translation facing each page of the original text.

110

The long-awaited volume — the textbook of Christian Science in Japanese — was completed in June, 1976. In the meantime, the Japanese edition of the Christian Science Quarterly had been prepared for July-August-September and it appeared just in time for use with the translated textbook.

Letters of gratitude poured in, describing the arrival of the textbook in Japan. These communications showed that the Japanese students who were not fluent in English had been waiting eagerly for this translation. These members were especially happy that now they could read *Science and Health* through in their native tongue instead of being limited to the few selected references from the Lesson-Sermon translations they had been receiving. They expressed gratitude even for the beautiful binding of the book and the choice of color for cover and jacket.

Since then, the impact of the translation has been more widely felt. Members have bought copies to give to friends, the book has been donated to many public and universtiy libraries, and each time an advertisement appears in a paper or magazine there is a happy increase of activity in the Reading Room.

Thinking back on this brief history of Christian Science in Japan, one marvels at the pattern of unfoldment. The twenty-five years

when Christian Science seemed to be kept in a
small group of Japanese families was a necessary time for planting the seed and watering it
to let the roots develop.

To one who has lived through the period,
it seems clear that it could only be God's gracious
plan that provided an unusual American educator and some wise and receptive Japanese mothers who saw the importance of having their
children learn English under this teacher's care.
When World War II broke out, members of the
Christian Science group not only survived it but
grew in their individual situations, and during
the Occupation years their horizons were greatly
expanded by their association with many fine
Christian Scientists from the United States.

This period brought about many fundamental changes in Japan. The entire educational
system was revised by the Occupying Army
Headquarters, and English became a compulsory
course in most schools. Democracy, if only on
the surface, was introduced in all phases of life.
The postwar young people have grown up liberated in a large measure from old Japanese
traditions and beliefs. The former binding
family structures and class distinctions according to wealth and background are not known to
many of these youths.

Having lost an established tradition to
follow, these young people began to look for

112

their identity. Freed from family religions, they were thrown among countless new faiths which were trying to catch their attention. Some of them have found Christian Science. In some cases, American friends have told them of it and have brought them to the church services; the attraction of the English language has brought others to visit the church; a gift of the Japanese edition of *The Herald of Christian Science* caused one young man to look into this teaching; another student, disgusted with the proselytizing methods of an aggressive new religious cult, was attracted by the simple, unassuming advertisement of First Church of Christ, Scientist, Tokyo, in a Japanese-English magazine.

These young people saw the necessity of learning English in order to study Christian Science. Many of them went to American colleges, especially Principia College, where they learned a good deal more than the English language. A number of them have attended the College Organization Conferences and the Youth Meetings held in Boston. These experiences have given them a warm and natural sense of being members of The Mother Church. They have expanded their friendships internationally, and they communicate well in English with young people from various countries.

It has been especially heart-warming to see the Asian Christian Scientists mingle with

113

each other. At one gathering, there were Indians, Indonesians, Koreans, Chinese, Filipinos, and Japanese, all happily exchanging in English their experiences as Christian Scientists. On the way home from Boston, several of the Asian students visited their fellow Christian Scientists' homes in Tokyo. Such encounters foretell the bright promise of our movement worldwide.

Then, too, several young American Christian Scientists who speak Japanese quite well have gone to Japan to teach English. It is impressive to see these bilingual youths working together and quite freely sharing their religion with Japanese inquirers.

Most of the young Japanese who have come into Christian Science have become active church workers in Japan or in the States. Many in this group have taken class instruction much sooner in their experience than the earlier Christian Scientists, who were timid about taking this step until they were sure of their understanding. The entire group of Japanese Christian Scientists who started out in the Tokyo church represent more than 20 different Christian Science Students' Associations in the United States, Great Britain and Indonesia.

In most cases, these students came into Christian Science without knowing much about the Bible. However, through their regular study

of the Bible-Lessons, they have been led naturally into understanding the mission and example
of Christ Jesus and to learn to demonstrate in
some measure the words of Mrs. Eddy in
Science and Health (p. 344):

> "There are various methods of treating dis-
> ease, which are not included in the com-
> monly accepted system; but there is only
> one which should be presented to the whole
> world, and that is the Christian Science
> which Jesus preached and practised and
> left to us as his rich legacy."

The translation of Christian Science
literature has proved to be a great help to the
Japanese. However, translation of *Science and
Health* in any language can be only as good as
the present understanding of the translators
chosen for the work from the Christian Scientists in their country. All translations, conse-
quently, are subject to future revisions as a result of the spiritual progress that comes with a
deepened understanding of the original text by
Mrs. Eddy.

However, the translation of *Science and
Health* surely is a sign of the seed showing its
sprout. An officer of The Mother Church who
himself has visited Japan and talked with Christian leaders there as well as with Christian Scientists wrote the author of this little memoir
after reading it in manuscript:

"It seems to me there is a parallel between the early beginnings of Christian Science in Japan, and the present new era, marked by the translation of *Science and Health* and the future this is ushering in. You bring out how Christian Science began there as a tender plant; how it was carefully nourished by Miss Boynton and the early Scientists; how this was really quite a challenge because of the surrounding cultural environment; and how the opportunities for a wider introduction were brought by the occupation and American influence.

"But aren't we seeing, in this present transitional period, with *Science and Health* just beginning its work in Japanese society in its translated form, a beginning somewhat like those very early days when two families were beginning to learn of Christian Science? It seems to me that our present translations work, with such achievements as the Indonesian and Japanese translations, is also a tender plant in a much, much larger garden. I see it as our present somewhat groping effort to prove a tremendous fact that inevitably will and must be proved — namely, that because the Truth revealed in Christian Science is *universal,* it is for all men everywhere, of whatever culture, and thus it must be translatable into terms that can be acceptable in cultures totally different from the Occident . . .

116

"Knowing the fundamental fact that the Truth of Christian Science is universal, we can look toward the future and see its promise. What was done in the Japanese translation is a symbol of this promise — the opening of a new door, and a hint of what can and will come."

The spiritual message of the Bible had been partly lost over the centuries through inadequate translations. How deeply significant is the provision made by Mrs. Eddy that the English of her writings always accompany any translation. And how blessed we are to live in an age when the language of the original text is within reach for anyone to learn!

The early Japanese Christian Scientists have left this precious legacy to the future generations.